Writing to Persuade

Writing to Persuade

How to Bring People Over to Your Side

TRISH HALL

LIVERIGHT PUBLISHING CORPORATION
A Division of W. W. Norton & Company
Independent Publishers Since 1923
NEW YORK • LONDON

Printed in the United States of America
First Edition

For information about special discounts for bulk purchases, please contact
W. W. Norton Special Sales at specialsales@wwnorton.com or 800-233-4830

Manufacturing by Lake Book
Book design by Ellen Cipriano
Production manager: Anna Oler

Library of Congress Cataloging-in-Publication Data

Names: Hall, Trish, author.
Title: Writing to persuade : how to bring people over to your side / Trish Hall.
Description: First edition. | New York : Liveright Publishing Corporation, a division of
W.W. Norton & Company, [2019] | Includes index.
Identifiers: LCCN 2019005692 | ISBN 9781631493058 (hardcover)
Subjects: LCSH: English language—Rhetoric. | Persuasion (Rhetoric)
Classification: LCC PE1408 .H3134 2019 | DDC 808/.042—dc23
LC record available at https://lccn.loc.gov/2019005692

Liveright Publishing Corporation, 500 Fifth Avenue, New York, N.Y. 10110
www.wwnorton.com

W. W. Norton & Company Ltd., 15 Carlisle Street, London W1D 3BS

1 2 3 4 5 6 7 8 9 0

To my teachers

CONTENTS

PART IV: TIPS ON WRITING

PART V: THE PSYCHOLOGY OF PERSUASION

PREFACE

For almost five years, as the person in charge of Op-Ed for *The New York Times*, I was immersed in argument, in passion, in ideas. I oversaw a dozen editors who read submissions from both the august and the unknown, all eager to be heard. Two assistants, looking for gems, pored over the hundreds of unsolicited manuscripts that arrived each week. I too read many pieces, a number so high that I never counted it. There was no time.

I was grateful for that perch, for the chance to know writers and editors who amazed me with their knowledge and creative minds. But I was also surprised by the flood of terrible writing from the famous and successful. Manicured products of Ivy League schools offered tangled sentences and mundane musings. People whose novel ideas deserved a hearing could not escape their jargon long enough to reach an audience.

At first this sea of opinion—from people eager, desperate even, to get their point across, to enter the flow of argument—was foreign to me. I had always been a journalist with no case to make, no argument to win. Whether I was reporting or writing or editing, and over the years I did all three, I was happy to absorb the thoughts and feelings of others. I had no interest in presenting my own point of view. I often thought I had no point of view, because early on I recognized a disconcerting tendency to be a chameleon, to use whatever was convenient from my past to make a connection with my subject.

Was I trying to bond with a working-class mother from the South? Then I would talk about growing up in rural Pennsylvania and how my stepfather had a dog kennel, and wasn't it funny how the dogs would bark every day at five, as if they were announcing cocktail hour? Was I interviewing a professor at Harvard? I would mention that my father had gotten his master's degree at Harvard, ten years before he moved to Los Angeles. I could be rural, urban—whatever suited my purposes.

I hadn't arrived in Op-Ed with an academic bent or experience on a journal of opinion and argument, as some others had. Opinion was a new world to me, and a frightening one at first. Over time I realized how lucky I was. The job gave me a chance to listen to America's feelings and thoughts, and do my best to help people reach an audience. If an idea spoke to me, whether from the right or the left, or even from no political persuasion, I was sure it would speak to others.

In *Writing to Persuade*, I hope to pass on to you what I have learned about writing and editing. I want to help you get your point across *in a persuasive way*, whether you are crafting an op-ed, a paper for a professor in college, an email seeking a job, or even a note to your husband. Although the book is mostly about writing, I occasionally wander into some of the psychology underlying these approaches. Knowing about human behavior is also useful when communicating face to face.

So, you might ask, are there rules for argument, for persuasion, for convincing people that they should listen to you? Yes, there are. Although it's challenging to change minds, there are fundamentals of persuasion, techniques for bringing people over to your side not only in written arguments, but in life. Like so many rules, they aren't easy to follow. And like all rules, they can be successfully broken. You could violate all of these concepts and still persuade someone to see your point of view. But be assured that using these methods, which require artistry, technique, and an understanding of human psychology, will increase your odds of success.

Here then are fifteen principles that I've come to rely on over my career.

Fifteen Principles of Persuasive Writing

1. Listen to people. The importance of thinking about your audience might be the most salient point I can make. Despite our culture of selfies, persuasion is not about you; it's about them. Whether you are engaging in a one-on-one conversation or attempting to convince the readers of a publication with millions of subscribers that they should listen to you, the first and most crucial step is to listen to them. You need to know who they are and how they feel.

2. We believe what we believe. Understand that we all cling to our opinions, for all kinds of good reasons. If you tell people something negative about their favorite candidate, they might become even more supportive of that candidate. They've already invested in that opinion, and it's not easy to get them to back away. These people aren't stupid. You're like that, too—you just don't know it. Is there a point where it's just not worth trying to reach those who don't agree with you? Of course. Sometimes you can't change people, and you have to accept that.

3. Respect your audience. Learn to be empathetic. Try to understand what it feels like to be them, to live their life. That's not easy, but it is essential.

4. Don't get into fights. Mostly, arguing doesn't work. People become defensive or they just tune out. The only people who might respond positively to battering and bullying are the much maligned workers in customer service who have no choice but to accept aggression. Don't say things like "You're wrong," or "I'm right and you know it."

5. Play on feelings. Feelings are crucial, much more important than facts. As Richard Friedman, a psychiatrist and professor in New York, puts it, "You have to use facts almost medically; you need to understand the mental and emotional state of your target audience to determine the right dose." We all respond to information that is emotionally engaging.

6. Understand moral values. Our moral values shape our interpretation of the world. You can get attention for your point of view only if you approach audiences with *their* values in mind, not yours.

7. Emphasize your similarities. People are more likely to agree with people who are similar to them. Likeable people are better than unpleasant people at persuading others to do what they want them to do. Be positive; be personable. Admit when you're wrong. I've always found an apology or an admission of error, deftly applied, to be potent.

8. What do you know? Write about what *you* know, in an area where your expertise is uncontested. If you're a computer technician, write about hardware or software. If your father is dying, and you're outraged by how the medical system deals with end-of-life treatment, write about that. There will always be something that you know or feel, and that's what you should focus on.

9. Surprise your reader. Endless words and images compete for our attention. Whether you're writing an essay for a professor in college or asking a bank officer for an extension on your mortgage application, you need to stand out. Someone might have to read your writing, but no one has to like it. You have to make them like it. If you're trying to get published, you must add a new idea to the conversation. Otherwise your work will just get lost, and there's no point in making the effort. Make it relevant, and something urgent, whether in fifty words or five thousand.

10. Be specific. If you make your point vivid—a twist in language, a startling idea—people will pay attention and be less likely to zone out. If you write in generalities and fail to use concrete, tangible details and images, your work will fall flat.

11. Tell stories. We all respond to stories. They're not a replacement for facts; without them, though, the facts will seem dull and dry.

12. Facts aren't magic. Facts won't convince people. People hear what they want to hear, and even the best, most perfect facts in the world will not change that. Indeed, we are capable of labeling anything we don't want to hear as "fake news." We take in facts selectively, sometimes unconsciously. I promise you, we all do it, regardless of our education or political beliefs. On their own, facts might not be as persuasive as you would like them to be. A startling one, though, can be the basis for a great essay or paper.

13. Facts do matter. If you make mistakes, you will be called out, and your writing will be mocked, discarded, or worse. Check your facts carefully. Mishandled, they will sink you.

14. Abandon jargon. Some of the smartest ideas have been smothered by jargon. Don't use it. Root out clichés. They feel canned and readers skip over them.

15. Prune ruthlessly. Most people use too many words. Trim, trim, trim. Many excellent books have been written on writing techniques, including four of my favorites, *The Elements of Style* by Strunk and White, *On Writing Well* by William Zinsser, *Draft No. 4* by John McPhee, and *Bird by Bird* by Anne Lamott. No one has ever learned all there is to learn about writing, so it's worth reading all of these books, and more. To write well, read omnivorously. Those who read constantly tend to write coherently.

PART I

Lessons from My Story

1

Becoming a Writer

Some people write because they need to do it for work or school and then discover that they like doing it. Others carry out research they find so compelling that they want to share their results with others. But some people have just always felt they were born to be writers, often for emotional and psychological reasons. It doesn't mean they're better, just that they chose their identity early. That was my trajectory.

I had every material advantage as a child. But like many children, I was often miserable. To escape, I read. I don't remember reading in the ranch house my parents built on a dirt road in northeastern Pennsylvania. I must have, though, because I lived there until I was almost eight, when my father ran away to California with the woman across the street, who was also the mother of my friend Fred. After that, we moved into my grandmother's house about five miles away, at the end of a dead-end street and close to a golf course lush with woods and streams. Nearby was a gypsy encampment, or at least we kids liked to believe that. When I wasn't roaming around outside or lying under the trees reading, I would take the half-hour walk into the center of the small town of Dallas, Pennsylvania, which had but a single stoplight. I would sit at a restaurant counter and eat shoofly pie, a Pennsylvania Dutch dessert thick with molasses. Afterward, I would go to the library and choose some books. Of course, before I was old enough to walk to the library alone, my mother must have driven me. That's hard for me to picture, because I didn't do a lot with my mother.

I remember our regular visits to a Dolly Madison ice cream parlor in Wilkes-Barre, the small city about twenty minutes away. We usually went there after my mother put flowers on the graves of her parents. She and I liked the same flavors of ice cream: coffee and mint chocolate chip. That memory stands out because we had so little in common otherwise. She was an extrovert who loved parties and might have preferred a different kind of daughter, one who didn't read endlessly and talk rarely. I probably reminded her of the man who had emptied his side of the walk-in closet in the middle of the night while she slept. Since the library was on the way home from Wilkes-Barre, that must have been when I returned the three or four books I had read that week and took out three or four more. By the time I went to high school, I had read most of the books in the young adult section. It got me through my childhood and allowed me to imagine I wasn't growing up in a place that never really felt like home. It was too remote, and I was too alone.

Books took me to cities around the world, into the lives of characters that became more real than the people who surrounded me. Of course, now I understand that no place with people is dull; it was my failure of vision. When I talk to relatives who still live in Pennsylvania, I am eager for their stories of the judge who profited from harming children, of the family who lost almost all of its members in just a year. They are sad stories, real and deep, suffused with the kind of drama that I found as a child in books. No matter where you live or where you grow up, there are intriguing people, stories with emotional resonance, ideas that are startling. I didn't see that then, in my discomfort with small-town life.

Many children exaggerate the pain of their upbringing, and I was no exception. I haven't told you about the magical long summer nights when the kids on my street played a game we made up called "The Chase," an elaborate version of hide and seek that involved a jail. Or the times I entertained my friends with stories of the wild parties on that street, and the shoes that ended up in refrigerators. Or of my two brothers, my many close friends, weekend sleepovers, and parties at the roller skating rink.

Still, reading was what I loved, and so I wanted to be a writer. But I had no idea how to go about it. Most kids growing up in the country today are not isolated in the same way, because they have the web. They can stream movies that show characters like them. Dallas had no museums, and I didn't know anyone who listened to classical music. My most exciting cultural memory involved hiding in the back seat of the neighbor's car and sneaking into the drive-in theater to see *Butterfield 8*, a movie about infidelity based on the novel by John O'Hara. Little surprise that for decades, I was obsessed with books and movies about infidelity. When you look for the subjects that speak to you, that you feel compelled to write about, be sure to mine the world that created you.

When I was a child, few people deviated from the unwritten rules of small-town life. My mother, being a divorcée for some years, was unusual, as were her close friends Betty and Agnes, sisters who had never married. Most of the adults I knew were married and had several children. They worked in small businesses. Or they were dentists, or doctors. But *writers*? I thought all the writers lived in New York, and so early on, I wanted to move there.

I always loved New York, a place that magically appeared in my life a few times a year when I would go to the city for a night with my mother, my aunt, and my cousin. Jefie and I would get matching dresses—blue for her, pink for me—at Best and Co., a classic department store that no longer exists, and return to Dallas the next day. Sometimes we visited my mother's friend, who was single and worked at Saks Fifth Avenue. Except for the strange spots on her arms, she was the most exciting woman I had ever met: She lived alone in New York City. Those trips ended when I was quite young, but their influence remained. Some years ago, I happened to be in the elevator of the hotel where we always stayed, and its distinct smell reminded me of my childhood craving for New York and my need to escape.

Besides the library, I had Mrs. Shortz. She taught seventh- and eighth-grade English in the days when other professions weren't readily available to a woman who had graduated from a top college like Smith, a pinnacle for intellectual women and one of the "Seven Sisters." And that was lucky for me.

Mrs. Shortz would write on the blackboard, "Winston Tastes Good Like a Cigarette Should." I can still see her holding the chalk against the board and pushing her body into the words. Those words made her mad. They were the tagline for a ubiquitous advertising campaign begun in 1954, and she was enraged that the copywriters had used *like* instead of *as*, thereby threatening to ruin grammar for my generation.

(Winifred Shortz wasn't the only rigorous grammarian in my

What's the deal with *like* and *as*? When you have a clause with a verb in it use *as*: Winston tastes good, as a cigarette should. When you have a clause with no verb use *like*: Winston tastes like a good cigarette.

life. My father was an engineer, but he was adamant about proper speech. When my younger brother, Bill, began peppering his conversation with the phrase "you know," my father obnoxiously and aggressively kept saying, "No, I don't know." He despised verbal tics that ruined the flow of a sentence.)

Because Mrs. Shortz wanted to be sure her students were not among the lost grammarians, she assigned us one piece of writing each day. We had to show up with what she called a response. It didn't matter what we were writing about. We could produce just one sentence or as many as three. Our responses had to be good enough to read to the class. I loved that form. It was like a minuscule poem. I wish I still had what I wrote, as a window into the girl I once was. But it wasn't the content that was important—it was the training. One thought or feeling a day. That's a great exercise for anyone who wants to keep track of observations that can be mined later for longer pieces of fiction or nonfiction. My teacher's advice about brevity remains useful for any kind of writing. Tight doesn't mean dull. It means consciously choosing your words and your sentence structure. Go back over the words until you are certain the reader doesn't have to make undue effort to read, but can sink into the sentences like a bath. No friction.

Mrs. Shortz didn't laugh at me when I said I wanted to be a writer. She told me I could do it. Every writer should seek a mentor like her. With her as my inspiration, I started down that path. I wrote for my grade school yearbook (including an embarrassing essay with the title, "The Difference between Wisdom and Intelligence") and later for my high school newspaper. In college, when I felt lost on a huge campus, I went to the *Daily Californian* in the middle of my sophomore year at Berkeley. It helped me find a purpose, and it made me a journalist.

If you're in high school or college and suspect you'd like to write, join whatever publications exist or become part of a creative writing group. Start one if there aren't any. Writing partners and groups will force you to be open and help give you structure. Learn from the feedback. You never know who your best teachers will turn out to be. They're not necessarily older, nor professors. Michael J. Hall, who died young in a fall from a bridge in Saudi Arabia, was the demanding, energetic city editor at the student paper, which had a daily distribution of 40,000 copies. Michael barked orders and strove for perfect copy. We wrote on half pages of paper so he could easily shuffle them to get the facts in the right order. He put a pencil over his ear and took it out to make corrections, just like real editors at real newspapers.

He was my first role model. Where did he learn it? Who knows. Maybe from his summer internship with the Associated Press. Maybe from the movies. Although he was only twenty, he taught me the basics of newspaper writing. He sent me out on my first assignment, to interview a professor. When I got back to the office and sat down to write, I realized that I had lost my notebook. Michael made me call the professor and ask the questions all over again. I can't remember the professor, the department, or the story; but I do remember that when I found myself without my notes, I felt like a failure. Michael made me transform that failure into a success and turn out my first story for the college paper. If he hadn't forced me to do that, I might have just left and become a city planner or something. To some degree, finding people like Michael who can push you is simply luck. But you have your own part to play; you have to stick it out and not flee when things get too tough. I've done this plenty of times, so I understand the impulse.

Michael was building a staff, and I became a core member, working as a reporter and then an editor. I learned how to write fast, and barge into crowds and start asking questions. As an editor, I learned how to meet deadlines and work with different kinds of people, from the occasional contributors who would never be journalists to the guys in the print shop who had to train a new crop of student production editors each fall. I learned, too, about the challenges in journalism when the *Daily Californian* ran an editorial about People's Park, a university-owned lot that students and local residents had illegally turned into a park. The university reclaimed the land in a bloody battle that left one man dead and another blind. It was an intense, emotional time, and we at the newspaper thought that the university should be resisted. The editorial called for people to take back the park, and after it was published, another riot took place. Our paper was blamed for starting it, and the five of us who made up the senior editorial board risked being indicted.

Typically, I hadn't even voted on the editorial. I had abstained, because I was too busy working on the news to pay attention and give my opinion. But the majority of the editorial board had agreed to the editorial, and after that riot, the paper was kicked off campus and lost university funding. We became a big story in the Bay Area. Most articles written about the incident were wrong in major or minor ways. Names were misspelled; the details of what the newspaper wrote were distorted. It was illuminating and discouraging, given that those stories were being written by "real," adult journalists. That taught me an important and sad lesson about the truth: no one agrees what it is, but you have to do your best to get the details right. The experience also made me wary of being interviewed by journalists, which is pretty funny coming from someone who has been asking people questions for decades.

Like half the people on earth, I still dreamed of writing a novel. But I knew I had to make money somehow, so in my senior year of college, I sent job application letters to newspapers within 40 miles of New Haven, Connecticut, where my boyfriend would be studying for a master's degree in public health. I got answers quickly and took the first job I was offered. Although I lacked confidence, I had a lot of experience for a twenty-one-year-old. I had already been a stringer for the Associated Press as well as a reporter and editor for a prominent college newspaper. I was the first woman at Berkeley to cover a riot. Indeed, I covered them so often that I was assigned my own gas mask in case I had to run out of my apartment to cover a conflict and didn't have time to get to the office. A man with my experience probably would have headed for New York, but I followed my boyfriend and the path of least resistance. I'm glad I did. I don't think I could have handled the competitiveness of New York at that age. It might have crushed me.

My confidence grew over the next nine years. You, too, might find it worth starting with small outlets and working your way up rather than facing rejection from the toughest places and giving up altogether. After briefly working as a reporter in Danbury, I got a job as a copy editor in New Haven. I was glad the commute to another city was over, although I missed reporting. I hated being stuck in the office, editing obits and stuffing copy into pneumatic tubes that flew through an internal maze to the composing room where the newspaper was put together. Most of my peers were reporters, busy going in and out of the office to cover police and school board meetings. I was surrounded by men, most of them older. There were few women working as editors then. My boss, Mr. Granger—and yes, in those days we addressed our superiors that way—treated me kindly and respectfully, like a daughter. That wasn't true of all the men. New Haven had a high crime rate in the early 1970s, so the men insisted that if we women worked late—which I did—a man would walk us to our cars.

One night I headed to the elevator with an older male editor.

We got in. The doors closed. He looked at me and grinned and said, "I could rape you right now."

I could see his eyes crinkling with laughter behind his glasses.

I guess I gave a forced laugh in return.

But I didn't think it was funny. Less than a year later, a group of around twenty women who worked on the two newspapers in New Haven sued the company that owned them. We based our suit on a survey we did of salaries, not on some of the loathsome personal behavior. In those days, there wasn't even a phrase yet for those experiences, which we now call sexual harassment. The idea that victimizing people because of their gender should be illegal was not articulated until 1979, in Catharine MacKinnon's book, *Sexual Harassment of Working Women*. Although the emotion we felt at being mistreated surely generated some of our drive to sue, we based our argument for discrimination largely on the differential in salary. I found that a man who was just like me—early twenties, top college, and working as a copy editor—made 20 percent more than I did. I still think fondly of the women in my class-action suit and the men who helped us. It's important to bond with your colleagues, wherever you go and whatever your work might be.

Like the women depicted in the book *The Good Girls Revolt: How the Women of Newsweek Sued Their Bosses and Changed the Workplace* (2012), I was a "good girl" to the core, even as I was rebelling against the mistreatment of women and flaunting the short skirts, long hair, and sexual freedom that defined the women of my time. I found it hard to go to work and look at Mr. Granger's hurt face. He liked me, and I had turned around and complained that the men were being unfair. At the same time, emboldened by our lawsuit, we started to organize a union. One of the organizers was Dan Collins, who was a reporter on the afternoon *Register*, while I was on the morning *Journal-Courier*. We had a number of organizing meetings at Dan's apartment, which he shared with his wife, Gail. After one of our meetings, a pretty woman with long dark hair, pale clear skin, and a menthol cigarette in her hand walked into the room and said that she needed someone to come and work with her in the small news service she ran in Hartford. It was Gail. Knowing nothing about her, I jumped up and said I would do it. I knew that thanks to my political activities, my bosses hated me. I felt guilty leaving before the union vote, but I feared I would never get another chance to escape.

I spent two years in Hartford with Gail, just the two of us. She had a graduate degree in political science and had married young, unlike anyone else I knew. After briefly working for some Connecticut papers, she started her own business covering the government for publications that weren't big enough to have full-time correspondents in Hartford. We had around thirty client newspapers, and each week we produced at least one story—often more—for each of them, about how they might be affected by pending legislation. We worked from 8 in the morning until 10 or 11 at night, at battered desks on the fifth floor of the state capitol building. We interviewed legislators, sat in on hearings, and wrote our articles, editing one another. For the first time since college, I loved journalism. Gail's relentlessly upbeat way of living and working would have been annoying if she hadn't been so funny. She never got discouraged, and she never got tired. She was one of the best bosses I ever had, and we became lifelong friends. Never underestimate the influence that friends have on your life. If you choose to hang around with slothful or cranky people who mostly watch television, you're likely to take on their habits. Gail was far more ambitious and positive than I was, and I am certain that her good traits influenced me and in the process made my life easier and more exciting.

She edited my work quickly and smartly, never making her criticism personal, always wanting the writing to be good. It was all that mattered—the work. That job taught me that I could write and write and write, work long hours, and get up at 7 a.m. to work some more—and be happy. I wasn't looking around and comparing myself to someone else my age, thinking that she or he was getting ahead faster or making more money. I thought only about what would happen each day inside that building, what the legislation meant, who was voting how and why. I was fascinated by the minutiae of government.

Each morning I carried cooked oatmeal and bags of raw broccoli into the building so I wouldn't have to waste time going out for food. We were bloggers before the internet, churning out stories, chain smoking at our desks just outside the office of the Committee for Public Health and Safety. Those were the days when many people smoked, and they smoked inside. We shared the space with some radio guys. I always thought that our being exiled to the top floor, away from the main press room, helped us develop a different perspective on the news. We weren't part of the pack.

After two legislative sessions, it was time to move on. Gail was a big proponent of tackling new challenges. I would have disappointed her if I had decided to stay. She helped me get a job as the editor of the *New Haven Advocate*, a weekly arts and news publication—in those days, they were called alternative papers. Throughout my life, Gail has helped me; and when I could, I have helped her. It's critical to find colleagues who will become both friends and mentors. Even in your early twenties, you are developing a professional circle that will help support you through the ups and downs of careers.

After a year, I decided to leave the *Advocate* for an editing and writing job at *Connecticut* magazine. A year later, just before turning thirty, I felt ready to move to New York, the place that had drawn me since childhood but also frightened me. It seemed less daunting than it once had, and I knew it was the next logical step in my life.

Again I thought about writing a novel, but I was unable or unwilling to make that leap. It seemed so lonely and hard. And I wanted to prove myself in journalism. Some painful failures, ever present in my brain, were pushing me along. I wanted to show those who had rejected me that they had made a mistake. One particularly bitter blow came from a top editor at *The New York Times* who had told me, after my weeklong copyediting tryout, that I would never make it on a big-city newspaper. The other dismissive comment came from the managing editor in New Haven, who claimed he could look around a room and know who would make it. I knew he didn't include me in that assessment, and the fury I felt about him was always present. How did he know I couldn't do it? It was a pleasure, years after our first EEOC discrimination complaint, to get on a witness stand and testify against the company knowing he was in the audience. We won our suit. Although the back pay wasn't huge after legal fees, it did help me freelance and pay rent on an apartment—albeit one populated by hundreds of cockroaches and attended to by a superintendent who stole all my jewelry.

I soon got a job writing for AP radio on a midnight to 8 a.m. shift. There I would read through page after page of news and turn the most important stories, no matter how long, into three sentences each. In some ways it was an awful job, putting me at odds with the normal social calendar; I slept all day and sometimes had a few beers at 8:30 in the morning after work. More than once, someone moved away from me on the subway. But to me, the job was thrilling. It was my entry into New York, and I learned so much from the discipline of reading the news and distilling it, much as I had when writing responses for Mrs. Shortz. No job is worthless if you can mine even one useful skill that will help you later.

After less than a year, I got a chance to do a tryout for an editing job at the *Wall Street Journal*. There was no reason to think I would succeed at the *Journal* when I had failed at the *Times*. The only economics course I took at Berkeley was called "A Critique of Capitalism and a Vision of Socialism." But that time, I passed. The lesson is obvious: you must persist, even if you get rejected. Sure, there are people who seem to have all the luck, who breeze from one great job to another. But I wasn't one of those people. I always felt like what people in my parents' generation called a late bloomer. But I've seen, over time, that the happiest people are those who work hard and take risks. I don't know where I got that willingness to fail. Maybe it was from being the ignored middle child in a family with a dazzling older brother and an adorable little one. Could be anything. But I was so relieved, so vindicated, so happy.

My job at the *Journal* was to edit and, if necessary, rewrite pieces intended for what we then called the "Second Front," the page for newsy features. That job gave me courage and finally made me realize my value, because I quickly discovered that some of these people working at a top paper in New York couldn't write as well as I could. That helped me shake off the shy girl from Dallas, Pennsylvania. Emboldened, I asked my boss if I could become a reporter. He explained that I had been hired as an editor, and such a switch was uncommon. But I wanted to write, needed to write, and he gave me a sliver of hope by saying that if I did some stories, maybe there was a chance.

In my own time after work, I started reporting a story about John Waters, the filmmaker whose raunchy, campy movies were cult hits. I aimed the story for what we at the *Journal* called the A hed, the spot on the front page for quirky, funny stories about things like pet psychics, chanting for success, and the trend of dirty hair. Waters was helpful and fully available, letting me follow him all day and visit his apartment in Baltimore, where he kept an electric chair. The story took me many weeks. I watched all of his movies, read everything written about him, then wrote and rewrote. But finally, it was done. When I was thirty-two years old, I had a story on the front page of the *Wall Street Journal*.

No one could dismiss me as just a writer for a small-town newspaper. Mrs. Shortz was right. I could be a writer. I *was* a writer.

2

Becoming an Editor

After the euphoria of that byline, I still had to show up every day between 10 and 6 and edit the words of other people. Was it my day job, or did I love it? I wasn't sure. Was I meant to be a writer, or not? As John McPhee makes clear in *Draft No. 4: On the Writing Process* (2017), writing is a torment, especially when doing the first draft.

If you procrastinate and think your work is terrible and yet are convinced that you want to write, you're not alone. Despite the agony, the upside of writing is big. The glamour goes to writers. No one ever says, when she gets a compliment on a big story, "Oh, this was junk until my editor got ahold of it." Good editors are scarce, and it is important to your own writing to seek out people whose feedback will make you better, just as you should embrace any teacher who pushes you to improve. There is endless craft in both writing and editing.

Although writing drew me, editing seemed easier to me than reporting, and there was less competition for the good jobs. The advice that you simply follow your bliss isn't always realistic and needs to be paired with an understanding of what the world will

A finance expert might write this in an article about the economy:

> Following the global reflation and synchronized global growth upturn of the past year, many believe that a normalization of the global economy is underway, with the U.S. leading the way out of those structural doldrums.

A business editor might simplify it to say this:

> Many people think that the global economy, led by the United States, is flourishing and that we have returned to normal following the 2008 recession.

actually pay you to do. Not that I was a born editor. Anyone who can't stop reading and writing is likely to be a decent editor, but everyone needs teachers, and my best editing teacher at the *Journal* was Fred Zimmerman. He demanded relentless editing, the kind it took to make the paper both sophisticated and easy to read. We had to deconstruct complicated ideas until they were understandable yet not distorted. We rewrote and rewrote and rewrote, referring to a list of words that Fred never wanted to see in a story because they had become clichés or were meaningless business babble.

I was terrified of displeasing Fred. He had given me no reason for confidence. When he hired me, he said that he wasn't sure I could do the job. He would let me try, and if I failed, I would be out. No surprise that I was scared. But I watched and I learned. After

Be mindful of using business jargon, which includes words like these:

- end user
- win-win
- verticals
- thought leaders
- scalable
- synergize
- disrupt
- pivot
- curate
- drill down
- incentivize
- core competency

You can improve your communication by giving these tired words a rest:

- monetize
- optimize
- impactful
- paradigm
- bandwidth
- mandate
- compelling
- momentum
- innovate
- dynamic
- literally
- influencer

I revised a story, he would go over it, fixing anything out of order, cutting out jargon and overused words—anything he did not consider conversational language. Because of Fred, I still cringe when I see *grow* used as a transitive verb, or *utilized* when *used* would do. In writing anything, avoid tired words and jargon. I thought of Fred recently when I read that the owner of an East Village bar was going to throw out any customer who used the word *literally*. It was meaningless, and he'd had enough.

Reporters at the *Journal* worked hard, but some of them relied on jargon or presumed too much knowledge on the part of the reader. Business reporting is a tough job. Interviews with executives as well as official materials and press releases were always larded with words intended to obscure reality. Companies rarely told reporters that they had laid off people, lost money, been caught misrepresenting their numbers, or been sued for something despicable.

We editors were fierce about eliminating jargon and making complex business and financial ideas understandable to readers so they did not have to struggle to get through the stories. As editors we made sure the writing was tight not because that was "better" in some abstract way, but because we knew a business reader wanted to get information quickly and efficiently. At the *Journal*, I learned the value of understanding your audience. Executives were busy people. Plus, we were what we called the second read. Our readers were buying other papers as well and would drop us if we didn't prove our worth.

I liked working with reporters and manipulating their words, but I missed the experience of encountering strangers and asking them questions, digging into their lives. And of course there was the lure of having your name out there, of being known. So on the side, I continued to write stories; and after three years as an editor, I became a reporter at the *Journal*. I covered food, alcohol, and tobacco, a beat meant for the less financially astute. That assignment suited me, and three years later, it led to a job reporting on food at the *Times*.

Maybe I'm just inherently restless. Even blessed with what

seemed a dream job—reporting and writing about food and chefs, going to wine tastings and fancy restaurants—I was drawn back to editing. If editing is the path for you, it's probably because like me, you enjoy the challenge of making something as clear and as simple as possible without distorting the meaning. It's fun.

And so I found myself running food coverage at the *Times*. Each editor transforms the publication he or she leads. I can always tell when a website or publication gets a new editor, because that editor's biases and interests are reflected in what runs, even as most editors remain invisible while the writers are known. I was interested in sociology and in nutrition, and the section reflected my taste. During my tenure readers got many more stories about eating habits and studies on the healthiest food choices. Other *Times* food editors have been more interested in chefs and recipes. All valid approaches.

As I grew into being both an editor and a manager, I tried to be different from the bad bosses I had had. One important lesson I learned from them: Don't be domineering, but do be decisive. There's nothing worse than a boss who can't or won't explain what she wants. Or one who waits forever to let you know whether to go ahead with a certain project or idea. Or just as bad, one who won't listen to other points of view and forces employees to carry out weak ideas that reflect her whims. When you're stuck with a bad boss, you have to maintain your passion for the work and force yourself to move ahead while knowing you also need to keep your supervisor happy. It's a tough situation. Probably the best decision, when you work for someone who isn't helping you learn or develop, is to find a new job.

I liked being in charge; and day to day, I liked editing more than writing. Writing was agony, especially when it involved facts. I never wrote a story without worrying endlessly about whether I had gotten something wrong. That thinking probably began during my college days, when I saw how even good reporters mangled facts. Those who knew would *know.* I worried even after I had gone over every word and checked it to be sure that it was correct.

I found editing relaxing, like the reading that filled my childhood. While my father and brothers had played bridge, I mostly sat in a corner chair, reading. When my stepmother did crossword puzzles, I was mystified. I tried, but just found them frustrating. Editing was my version of a crossword puzzle or bridge. It was a game, a mental activity that did not come with terrifying stakes, like reporting.

At least, that's what I thought until I was put in charge of the Op-Ed section of the *Times.*

3

Running Op-Ed

I couldn't sleep that night.

What if the article I was about to publish by Vladimir Putin wasn't from Putin? What if it was a hoax, something that would humiliate me publicly and lead to my firing? As a child I used to daydream about accepting awards for my novels. As an adult, my daydreams were more like nightmares. I worried about my dog being run over by a car. I worried about my daughter being attacked on a deserted street. Now, I imagined that the hoax that had trapped me would be the top story the next day in the gossip and media site Gawker, ending my career.

In my restless wide-awake state, refreshing my email obsessively in a darkened bedroom while my husband slept, I relived the day. I had received an email from a public relations executive I had never met who said he worked for a large international firm in Brussels, that he represented the Russian head of state, and that he had an op-ed to offer. Putin! He never wrote for the American media. I said, "Sure, I'll take a look."

> I am partial to short first sentences—even when they make up the entire first paragraph. They're easy to take in. Make them a little twisted, a little surprising, so the reader wants to continue.

An hour or so later, the piece arrived. I mostly liked it, although some of its points might have been considered not quite true. In consultation with our lead fact-checker, I asked for some wording changes to protect us from being deluged the next day with complaints of, "That's not right."

Putin's representative insisted that the Russian leader had written the article and was attached to each word, so he couldn't just go ahead and say yes to anything. Could that be true? Could one of the most powerful, most feared men in the world be in his palace stretched out on a couch, hard at work on a laptop, writing his op-ed? Because Putin's representative couldn't approve changes, the time difference meant that editing moved slowly. Each time I asked for something as small as removing an *a* or a *the*, I would get an email saying, "I'll have to get back to the Kremlin on that."

I would like to have talked to Putin. Ever since immersing myself in Russian novels in high school and taking Russian in college, I had been intrigued by that part of the world. Sadly, I just had a lot of emails back and forth with his people, until just before our 9 p.m. print deadline.

I never did call the people who the public relations executive had suggested could vouch for the op-ed's authenticity. My boss,

Before considering logic, structure, and spelling, an editor should think about the overall truth and authenticity of a piece of writing.

- Get the name of any unidentified source. Does the writer have any history with that source?
- Does the writer know any of the people being quoted?
- Does the writer have any possible conflicts of interest—an investment in the company being written about, a relative who works there?
- Research the writer to be sure you know about anything that might make you hesitate to publish the work.

Andy Rosenthal, who had once worked as a correspondent in Moscow, had received a call from the *Times* reporter there. The reporter told him that Putin wanted to submit an article. That seemed like enough validation of the Russian president's identity. Calling people I didn't know who could be pretending to be someone they weren't seemed like a mistake.

As that sleepless night refused to end, I kept telling myself that I had obtained plenty of confirmation for the authenticity of the piece. Even so, I worried that I should have done more. To take my mind off of the certain Putin disaster, I decided that 3 a.m. New York time was the perfect moment to start answering emails from our Hong Kong bureau. Besides, how was I supposed to rest when in the same room a man and dog snored in unison, happily sleeping while my career collapsed before me like a crumbling hillside?

That was a particularly scary day, but it wasn't the only one. Journalism is brutal. In surveys, most people say they mistrust and dislike journalists. After decades in the field, I'm still not sure why anyone thinks they could do it better.

Journalism is exhausting. You're constantly swept up in deadlines. You're criticized by your bosses, by readers, by media critics and columnists. You have a lot to lose at all times. The pay is low considering that a reporter needs a college degree as well as fluency with interviewing, writing, and analysis—and for those skills makes on average about $52,000 a year. Reporters at big-city unionized papers like the *Times* make twice that or more, but they're a small part of the workforce.

Getting the Op-Ed job was random, as many things are. I had heard that David Shipley was leaving his job as the Op-Ed editor to start an opinion operation for Bloomberg. I already had a great job, and I felt grateful to have arrived on the newsroom masthead as the editor in charge of the feature sections. Even though my job sounded important, it felt inessential to me. If I took two weeks off, the work would continue as before. I wanted to edit and make decisions about what stories appeared in the paper and on the site, not just manage people. So I wrote Andy Rosenthal an email asking, "Would it make any sense at all for me to apply for this job?" If he was going to hire someone from *The New Yorker* or the *Atlantic* I wanted to know, before I got too excited. He answered immediately.

"Sure. Come up and talk to me."

We're all nervous before interviews, if the stakes are big. But there are ways to calm yourself. If you're prepared with the facts you need to be persuasive, that show you're the right person for the job, then it's much easier to relax.

In the few days before the interview, I immersed myself in what Op-Ed had been publishing and then headed up to the thirteenth floor, where I found Andy. With his flyaway hair, jagged beard, and a shirt from Target, he was obviously indifferent to labels and style, so I felt comfortable right away. He was sitting in a corner office with views west to New Jersey, where he was proud to live. I sat down on the gray couch where I was to spend so much time in the next five years.

It was a relaxed and intriguing conversation. He was quick and funny and smart, and I felt like I was talking to a friend I hadn't seen in a long time. The next morning, I sent him a long note recapping some of the story ideas I had mentioned and explaining why I thought I was the right person for the job. After you meet with someone you're trying to influence in some way, always send a follow-up note thanking the person for taking the time to talk, and use the email as a way to take the conversation even further.

I should have been thrilled when he offered me the job, but I almost said no because the leap from news to opinion seemed too big. After hours of conversation with a close friend and fellow journalist, I decided I would and could do it. He convinced me that Andy wanted what I had to offer: a relaxed way of working with people, broad experience in journalism, and just a trace of the nerd factor that sometimes drives away general readers.

The first day on my new job, I saw that I had been deluded in thinking I could make that leap. What had ever made me decide that this made sense? People were looking to me for direction, so of course I pretended that I was fine. I knew they admired their former

News organizations have multiple ways of reporting the news—through stories, profiles, features, graphics, videos, podcasts, and news analyses. Although the forms vary, they all are supposed to give perspectives from different people on what the story means. A story might say that a bridge fell down and twenty people died, and some people are blaming the mayor; but as contrast, it might also say that other people think the problems started long ago.

Opinion pieces are not like news stories. They have facts that must be verifiable, but they do not need to be balanced or give equal time to various points of view. There is always a conclusion or a solution—that bridge fell down because the government was incompetent, and the solution is to vote out the mayor and create a special agency to fix infrastructure.

boss. I wasn't following a failure; I was following a successful, well-liked editor. At the very least, I couldn't let the staff see that I was nervous and intimidated. But I had no idea what I was doing. And I do mean, no idea. Since becoming a journalist in high school, I had believed that I should always try to be fair and impartial. Suddenly I was charged with seeking opinions. Even with being opinionated. I didn't want to give my own opinions, and I didn't know what an opinion piece should be.

The *Times* and other publications run many types of stories, graphics, and videos, but all of them, when labeled as news, typically report what happened and attempt to bring together various important elements of a story and make sense of them; the opinion piece makes a strong argument without being forced to present other points of view. I had never written an opinion piece or thought about what made one successful.

I learned quickly though, mostly from the editors who worked for me, because I had no choice. They were an amazing crew, dissecting words and ideas with sustained rigor. Bosses don't admit often enough how much they learn from the people they are leading. In my case, some of those who worked for me were much younger, and yet their experience was more relevant than mine. I survived and flourished only because I absorbed their different thinking processes and editing styles. As each day went by, I developed an understanding of how to assess the strength of a potential op-ed by reading their responses in our internal email called Op Discuss.

Anyone in Op-Ed, from a young assistant to an experienced deputy, could send a piece to the Op Discuss address, and anyone could jump in and say what they thought. Should it run? No? Be revised? Those emails were priceless to me. As I looked at the comments from the staff, I began to remember what I had learned in high school and college about making an argument.

The approach to argument that I learned in classes at Berkeley was much more similar to an op-ed than the inverted pyramid of daily journalism or the slow, anecdotal flow of feature stories that had dominated my professional life. Despite their varying perspectives, the editors were bonded by the desire to get the most original thinking on every topic. Their responses were witty, smart, and taught me how to identify an article's logical flaws. That applied to the traditional eight-hundred-word articles we ran in print on the Op-Ed page as well as the long and less conventional work that made up our online offerings, which featured series on areas like philosophy, psychology, and the Civil War.

Not long after I started, I got a critical lesson in op-ed writing from Carmel McCoubrey, the editor who was the final reader on all copy. She heard me debating with another editor the pros and cons of asking a certain writer to contribute, and I think she was frustrated by our unfocused discussion. Looking annoyed, she stood up and made this pronouncement: It has to be a surprising idea or a surprising person writing. If you don't have either, it's not worth running.

Then she sat down. And with those words, she succinctly explained what Op-Ed editors are looking for.

Wherever you are, in school or at work, learn from the people around you. There are a variety of approaches to thinking and editing. All have something to offer. Mimic your smartest, most creative colleagues.

I tend to read and edit fast. I tell myself that my style puts me in the place of the busy reader. More likely I read fast because I just do, and I always have. My third-grade teacher wrote on my report card that I read too fast, and if that continued I wouldn't remember what I read. She was right! I don't remember much of anything and never have. But that's my style. I give writers fast answers; I go with my instincts about what should be at the top, what at the bottom, what is missing. I edit so quickly that all my editors knew that if they had something long that needed five hundred words chopped out on deadline with just 5 minutes before the close, I would be eager to dive in and do it for them.

Learn what you are good at and build on it, but also work on your weaknesses and study those who are different from you. My polar opposite in editing style was Aaron Retica. I hired Aaron from the *Times* magazine, where he led the fact-checking department and also edited stories. His mind was miles deeper than mine. He edited deliberately and slowly, answering writers with long queries about structure, language, and the like. He rarely changed the writer's words. He asked for rewrites, and kept asking until he was satisfied. Aaron withheld copy as long as he could, not wanting to release it until it was flawless. I had been trained on newspapers, which value speed, while he had worked for magazines and was rewarded for thinking more carefully about flow and structure.

So don't reject different styles. Learn from them. It is easy to dismiss them as inferior, but if you do, you will be missing an opportunity to improve. Same with backgrounds and perspectives. Aaron grew up in Manhattan, the child of working-class Italians and lower-middle-class Jews, and went to Yale; that informed his ideas, just as my small-town, WASP-y upbringing affected mine. Look for people who will round you out and present different points of view.

Gradually I merged what I considered my biggest strength—an affinity for different kinds of people and an understanding of what they might want to read—with this unfamiliar form of opinion writing, in some cases stretching the definition so it included whatever I wanted to read. Did I want to please the audience? Of course. But from my earliest days as an editor, I published what spoke to me. I don't know of any other way to work. You can't go by what people say they want, because they often don't know until they see it.

If you want to be an editor, you need to read widely. That's the only way you will recognize an original idea when you see it. There's another benefit, too: absorbing varied styles will turn you into a bit of a ventriloquist, so you will be able to help writers find their own voices.

Eventually, despite the endless hours and the feeling that the learning curve was not only steep but maybe insurmountable, I was glad I took the job. Beginnings are hard for a lot of us, so don't make rash decisions after your first day, week, or even month in a new job. Andy, who looked like a teddy bear, was a big part of the reason I was happy in my job. He was quick and funny, telling long stories about his life in Moscow, his time running the foreign desk, his years in Washington. He had a talent for supporting his staff when they needed him and leaving them alone the rest of the time. He had little respect for authority or conventional wisdom. Andy demonstrated the value in being original and refusing to follow the pack. He appreciated that quality in others, which is critical in a boss. I never felt that he would give me a hard time for doing surprising things. I never asked permission first before exploring some outlandish idea with a writer.

Andy had another rare quality: he actually liked women. With him it wasn't affirmative action, nor was it theories about the economic benefits of diversity. Until Opinion, I had never worked in an environment, other than the traditionally female ones like Style, that had so many women. I remember when I wanted to hire the opinion editor of the *Guardian*. Without knowing much about him, Andy was opposed, partly because he made too much money. But I thought it was more than that.

"Andy, you have to get over your aversion to men," I said. "It's not his fault."

He just raised his eyebrows. "We have enough men."

And he was right. Although there were many women in the

department, in the core group of Op-Ed editors, the ones who decided what we would run, men far outnumbered women. Women and men, coming from different backgrounds, bring different perspectives, as do people from different races, parts of the world, and social classes. I didn't disagree with Andy. At all. I had interviewed many women for the job, though, and no one seemed to me as good as the *Guardian* editor. I wanted variety in viewpoints, but the Op-Ed department had to churn out a ton of stories, and that was worrying me.

"We need someone like him," I told Andy. "He has a lot of experience, and he's fast and smart. So many of our editors are young. He balances it out." Eventually I prevailed, but only after agreeing to trim the salary of another open slot, which pretty much guaranteed it would go to a young person.

Whatever disagreements we had were couched in humor. I knew Andy had my back. When I landed in Op-Ed, I learned what it meant to be attacked all the time. If I ever forgot, all I had to do was look out the window at a big billboard outside of the *Times* put up by CAMERA (Committee for Accuracy in Middle East Reporting in America), complaining about our supposed bias against Israel. The kind of support Andy gave me is not something I've always had in a boss, and in your work life, it's worth searching out.

But there were limits. If the Putin story was fake, there would be no recovery.

That night, I was so exhausted from the tension that when I finally went to sleep, I overslept. I grabbed my phone when I woke up around 9 a.m. and opened my email, terrified, knowing that if something had gone wrong, it would be clear by now.

There was no story in Gawker. No angry emails. No problem.

And so another day began.

4

Dealing with Celebrities

Most of the time, famous people were trouble.

Politicians would promise pieces and then never file, giving no explanation. Celebrities resisted efforts to make their writing more concrete and specific.

You'd think, with all the money they spend on public relations experts, that their pieces would arrive in perfect condition. But that was rarely the case. They had the same problems making successful arguments that everyone has. The difference? They could go straight to the top. Their submissions never languished in a slush pile.

Famous people often started with my boss, Andy Rosenthal, or the publisher, Arthur Sulzberger. Andy and Arthur nearly always said the decision was mine, but I knew they would have to take responsibility for whatever I did. They never forced me to run anything I didn't want to run.

I remember one submission from a famous person that elicited the typical reaction from one of my editors: "This seems painfully obvious. But do we want it? For their names?" If you write something painfully obvious and you're not famous, your work will never make it out of the pile of unsolicited manuscripts.

When we decided against the piece, Andy said, "I'll just take the heat when it goes into the *Post* or the *Journal*." The next week, another famous man, another obvious piece. When I said no, which meant Andy would have to justify my actions, I experienced anew what a great boss he was. He never made me feel I had to take sub-standard pieces. He would turn it into a joke—in that case, emailing me back, "Heavy sigh. Why can't we be fabulously wealthy instead of having to deal with this?"

Some celebrities rejected us after we attempted to edit their work. They preferred to publish someplace that didn't demand so much of them or violate what they considered their essence. Famous people have no interest in getting a note back that says, "We would like to run this, but we need a rewrite; our questions are below." That just doesn't happen. They would rather take it somewhere else than go through that, and I don't blame them. They didn't have to pub-lish in the *Times*. Whatever they had to say would end up in front of people through social media. We needed them more than they needed us.

When I speak to students, professors, and others interested in opinion writing, they always want to know about the celebrities I have worked with. Yet that was my least favorite part of the job. We often had to reject their work, and that felt weird. I always had to tell myself that I was thinking of the reader. If I started running articles solely because of who the authors were, I would be lower-ing standards, and that would hurt the *Times*. I didn't want to dis-appoint readers with anything that seemed shallow or pandering.

Although they don't usually drop their subscriptions because of just one article, subscribers eventually will walk if quality declines.

Celebrities often fell into the trap of believing that they could say anything and it would be published. Maybe their handlers told them their names were enough to sell it, but that wasn't true. There has to be a point, and it has to be a surprising one, no matter your name or pedigree.

I remember having to reject a piece from Bono, the lead singer for U2, who had previously done a series of well-received columns as a contributing opinion writer. One September day, his public relations person emailed my boss saying that she wanted to chat. And yes, they always want to chat. Andy sent her to me, and as usual I too avoided the phone, asking her to just send the piece so I could share it with my editors. People think that personal contact will help; but many editors resist it because those calls take time and, in the end, are not why things get accepted or rejected. I found it useful to get to know writers only when they were regulars, and our coffee meetings were devoted to thinking of ideas for great pieces. It's your writing, not your contacts, that will make you successful.

When Bono's piece arrived, I sent it around without saying what I thought. One of the longtime editors, always civilized and succinct, had a reaction that summed up the problems quite well: "It feels too much like a guided tour of African despair—not surprising at 1,600 words. Maybe with a little more focus, much shorter?"

Others pointed out that Bono had violated a cardinal rule of writing an op-ed: Don't call for something that will never happen, like spending trillions on Africa. It's meaningless. Another editor thought the piece would grate on our readers, and he quoted a line from a 2005 *Times* Op-Ed piece: "There are probably more annoying things than being hectored about African development by a wealthy Irish rock star in a cowboy hat, but I can't think of one at the moment."

So, rejected it was.

A week later, a different public relations person got in touch with a draft of an op-ed, now from Bono and Mark Zuckerberg, the chief executive of Facebook. Were we ready to reject that duo? Just a week later? Again, the editors didn't like it. They criticized the piece as being "obvious," "painful," "self-serving." But they acknowledged the power of big names and the audience interest in them.

I decided to try. The article was tied to a speech that Zuckerberg was scheduled to give at the United Nations, which made it newsy. Maybe it could be saved. Or maybe I was just being a wimp, and too human? Had I used up all my willpower on the first submission? I wrote back to the public relations person saying that I needed a rewrite, and I gave him some suggestions on how to be more specific in a way that I thought would interest readers. He needed to think about what news they could create because, given the authors, the piece would be picked up by other news outlets. (You don't have to be famous to write an article that makes news. When Greg Smith quit his job at Goldman Sachs on the Op-Ed page with a critique of the firm's culture, the reaction was huge.)

In our editing, we asked Bono and Zuckerberg to say more than just that people needed digital access. How, we asked, do you manage that when hundreds of millions of people don't even have electricity? Shockingly, a short time later, they delivered a new, much better piece. It was more to the point and had specific answers to the questions we had posed. It was pruned of irritatingly vague suggestions, and we were happy to publish it. Despite being famous, these celebrities too had to meet the demands we made of all pieces: that they be surprising, concrete, and persuasive.

Particularly difficult were the pieces from accomplished writers and novelists. There was no question they could write, better than any of us could. But doing a bestselling nonfiction book or an award-winning novel is no guarantee of a successful op-ed. They are totally different forms.

I remember a piece from a famous novelist. It seemed, with some edits, like something we could publish. We made suggestions, and she sent back a revise through her representative. That version was better, but it still had some parts we didn't like because they were too promotional and sounded like an infomercial. It also took too long to get to the point. But as one editor said, "If she'll let us cut it right down, I vote yes."

We struggled to meet our standards and to make her happy. We knew we had to tread carefully, because we *did* want to publish her. I told her representative that we would edit her revised article and trim it to the length that suited our space. I didn't think we had anything drastic, so I was surprised and disappointed to hear a few days later that they were ditching us.

Politicians could be difficult, too. They would promise pieces and then fail to deliver. One time, the communications staff for Hillary Clinton offered something that they promised would be both long and important for our Sunday section, which meant holding open space that would be hard to fill if she failed to come through. Clinton's people were coy and wouldn't tell us what she was going to say, but we were game. Send it, we said, we're waiting.

And wait we did.

We waited. We emailed. They said it was coming. Then they said they needed a little more time. This was not our first experience with her communications staff. As the editor who was handling it wrote at the very beginning, "Let's just try to make sure they'll send it by 3 but don't send it until 6 and then pull it at 7:45 . . . just kidding."

Well, it happened again. Silence. Crickets. Nothing ever came, not even an explanation of why it wasn't coming.

Why? Because those things are group efforts, even though they appear under the name of one person. More people, more problems. The editor who had been burned was still willing to work with Clinton's people. He wrote, "I expect we'll get something sans apology around 8, and they'll be apoplectic when I tell them it's too late. Still, we should hold out for possibly running this hypothetical piece on Tuesday, assuming it exists and we like it."

Often people with power or fame just wouldn't respond to emails. They knew we needed them more than we needed us. Then they would say they wanted to move their piece to a different date, so we would go through the agony of waiting all over again. Or we would just never hear back, and see their piece with no edits in another publication, making the lesson clear: if you dare to ask questions or require edits, we will just go somewhere else, without even telling you.

While we were discouraged by how difficult it could be to edit people who were annoyed with our questions, we at least had one another. I remember the time a well-known academic was so obnoxious to an editor in a phone call that we all stood and cheered when she finally hung up. Don't be abusive; screaming never makes an editor want to bend to your will.

Of course we weren't mistreated by all celebrities. Sheryl Sandberg, the chief operating officer of Facebook, wrote a series of articles about women in the workplace with Adam Grant, the Penn professor who was one of our regular contributors. Adam was always a pleasure to work with—smart ideas, fast delivery—and his friend Sheryl was similar.

Occasionally, I was utterly wrong about people. In the spring of 2011, I headed toward my daughter's graduation from Kenyon College with hostile feelings about the graduation speaker. We would be hearing from Jonathan Franzen, whose novels I had deliberately never read. I had decided that life was too short to spend my time reading someone I believed to be a misogynist. In a well-publicized dustup, he had declined to go on Oprah Winfrey's show, implying that he didn't care about her all-female audience. I figured there were tons of novels I wanted to read, so why give my time and money to someone with disdain for people like me?

Like everyone, I can be stupid and bullheaded. I was wrong about him. His speech about technology and nature was so inspiring I shifted from being an enemy to a starstruck fan. When I got back to New York, I found Franzen's email in our system. After telling him how much I had liked his speech, I asked whether we could run it in Op-Ed. We didn't usually run speeches as essays, but I found his talk so remarkable I figured it was worth breaking the rule. He was lovely to deal with and easy to edit, not in the least condescending. I was, of course, humbled. I wondered how many other people in my life I had been wrong about.

PART II

What's Your Story?

5

Finding Your Voice

You don't have to be famous or powerful to offer something useful to the public conversation. We can all, with some work, find stories to tell. Well-known people have a better chance of being published—but only if they can figure out what their story is and how to tell it.

A few years into my new job as Op-Ed editor, I got an email from one of our columnists, Nick Kristof, informing me that the daughter of his friend Mia Farrow wanted to write a piece about the molestation she said she had suffered at the hands of her father, Woody Allen. Although Nick writes powerfully about suffering in the world and visits the poorest, most remote places, he also has some famous friends. I said I would take a look.

Most of Dylan Farrow's allegations were not new, but her piece was wrenching. It was her story, powerfully told. Still, I doubted I could run her article because by definition, an op-ed does not give the other party a chance to comment. It seemed unfair to run an article alleging a crime without getting reaction from Allen. I emailed my boss about it, saying my impulse was to pass. Because no investigators or court had brought a case against Allen, I thought we'd be in legal jeopardy. Andy agreed.

So I told Nick that we would have to reject it, and he informed the family. Shortly after, he asked whether he could run her story in his column. That seemed fine to me. It didn't have the same legal ramifications, because in his column, Nick could ask Allen for comment.

As soon as Nick's column ran, along with an expanded version of Farrow's story on his blog, I heard from Woody Allen's publicist. Her client, she said, wanted to write a piece for the upcoming Sunday section.

Polite discussions over timing, space, fact-checking, and the like ensued. Allen said he had much to say that had never been said. He would send the piece to me only if he could be guaranteed the same amount of space that Dylan Farrow's story had been given in Nick's column. I said fine, if the piece was worth the space. There was a pause in our email exchange after that; it made me wonder whether Allen had decided to go elsewhere. Was his publicist working with a publication that had offered her a better deal, with no qualifier that the amount of space devoted would depend on how interesting the article was?

So I wrote back, again: "Are you interested in sending something from Mr. Allen? Obviously we're very interested in seeing what he has to say."

While I worried that the publicist had ditched us, it was just the normal busyness of work and life; she was surely getting hundreds of calls on Farrow's piece. She promised to submit by the next morning. When the piece arrived, I read it instantly. Allen said that with this article, he was done, and would never again comment on the matter. It was powerfully written, in great detail. I said I had to run it by our lawyer, and then it would have to be fact-checked.

It was weird to be in the middle of a family conflict, although if you become an editor you will find it happens surprisingly often. We would run an essay by a son who talked about his falling out with his mother and then she would call, outraged, with a very different version of reality. One editor I know, when he was just starting out, had to sit through an endless lunch with one of his literary heroes while the man consumed nine scotches and revealed the details of his unsatisfying marriage and his impotence.

Was Allen innocent? Guilty? I could not tell. I was still a newsroom person at heart, without a lot of opinions. I just knew that he had never been charged, and I thought he deserved to tell his side because of the space we had given his accuser. Still, I knew that many readers would be furious. Was I going to let someone that many people considered a child abuser have space in Op-Ed?

Allen knew what story he had to tell, which is the first and most important step in figuring out what to write. He didn't offer a treatise on bitter divorces, or family feuds, and he didn't refer to the movies that have made him so well known. He was just writing about the particular experiences that his daughter had brought up, giving his point of view.

There will always be something you know or feel or observe that others do not. We are all individuals with a singular experience and sensibility. Your writing has to reflect that, whether you are eighteen or eighty, known or unknown. Plenty of famous people have tried and failed to write publishable articles because they haven't understood what story they have to tell.

I teach occasionally, and once worked with two dozen high school students in a course on opinion writing. They wanted to discuss the issues that were important to them—feminism, gay identity, Israel. I encouraged them to think about their personal, singular experiences in the context of those issues. No one cares what a high school student thinks about the path to peace in the Middle East. On the other hand, if that student spent part of the summer at a camp with both Palestinian and Jewish teenagers, her recollections might lead to a publishable, persuasive essay. That teenager would be telling her story, and her experience would make her an authority.

You must always have a clear reason to be telling the story you are telling, along with some expertise in that matter. Whether you feel confident or not, write with authority. Lay out your credentials. People are attracted to those who demonstrate knowledge on a topic. You don't need to have a doctorate. Just make it clear that you have the experience or the history to write about your subject, whether you are a struggling landlord in Cleveland or a young woman who decides to take off her hijab for a day.

Use your individual experiences to make points of universal interest. When you write the way you talk rather than the way you think people should write, you are being authentic. If you just give lists of facts or write the way "experts" write, you will not sound real. Adding emotion and concrete details—as the landlord did, pointing out that he bought eviction notices by the carton—amplifies your power. Sounding like a technocrat diminishes it. It's tedious to read words that sound like they could have been spit out by a robot. It is critical to write in your own voice. I know; that advice is tough to follow. It's like saying, "Relax!" It's about as useful as the advice my older brother gave me when I was thirteen or so and wanted to get the attention of boys. "Be yourself," he said. But it's true.

You need to strip out the external voices and allow your true voice to come out. There are a few tricks to that. Sometimes, when I can't get started, I write with my eyes closed, to block out reality. Other times I talk into my phone, and the voice memos help me get going on something that has been troublesome. No matter how you get there, you have to write from your deep self. If you stay at the level of your office brain or your academic self and use the jargon of your profession, you will kill your work. You might not even know what story you want to tell until you think about what you, and only you, can offer.

In one prescient piece I edited that preceded Donald Trump's presidency, a rich man in New York called on his fellow rich people to do something about inequality before the ever-growing income gap spawned a revolution or a popular uprising. In an op-ed titled "Capitalists Arise," which he later turned into a book, Peter Georgescu told the story that he knew and could tell: that his rich friends were scared. His first version didn't start out like that. It was more abstract. He wrote in generalities, about the big issues of the day. As we got to know each other through phone calls and email, I asked him to tell what he knew and tell it as directly as he could.

The result was an appeal to the nation's privileged from one of their own. It's possible that Peter understood how rapidly and devastatingly change could come because he had been born in Bucharest, Romania, and fled Communist rule. Although there's no way to know if he changed any minds with his article, as a

Here is an unedited piece followed by the version edited by EvidenceNetwork.ca, which helps academics in Canada make their work more accessible to the public. The first has no voice and feels robot-like; the second has voice and feels human.

BEFORE

Canada Post Corporation (CPC) is looking for a new President and Chief Executive Officer. Deepak Chopra, the former head of the Crown, stepped down in January.

The opportunity to run one of the largest and most significant federal Crowns is a daunting one. The new leader will have to manage a host of operational and structural challenges facing this firm and will have to do so in a deeply politicized environment. The Liberal government has, and looks to continue, to interfere in CPC's operations to meet partisan aims. He or she will need sharp political, business and diplomatic skills in order to steer CPC towards a sustainable future.

I offer the following observations: CPC's core purpose is to provide mail and package delivery services to rural areas and small towns—places where private sector logistics firms offer limited service. CPC is granted (or cursed, depending

refugee and the emeritus head of one of the largest advertising agencies in the world, he had the authority to suggest that people ought to view their wealth as not simply an unalloyed good. If that piece had been written by someone with a middle-class on how you look at it) with a national monopoly on mail service, but this does not cover the costs to provide remote services. CPC is obligated to serve all Canadian addresses, and this "Universal Service Obligation" must be met regardless of the cost.

AFTER

Looking for a new job? Canada Post is looking for a President and Chief Executive Officer. But it's not a position anyone should consider lightly.

The new CEO will face daunting challenges managing Canada Post's operational, financial, and governance deficiencies in this digital age, and will have to do so under close public scrutiny and in a deeply politicized context.

However mundane it might appear, mail delivery is politically significant to the federal government. Mail and parcel service is one of the few tangible things the federal government does which affects the daily lives of the general population. Any problem with mail delivery makes its way swiftly to our elected MPs. Instances of poor customer service or corporate mistakes generate newspaper headlines.

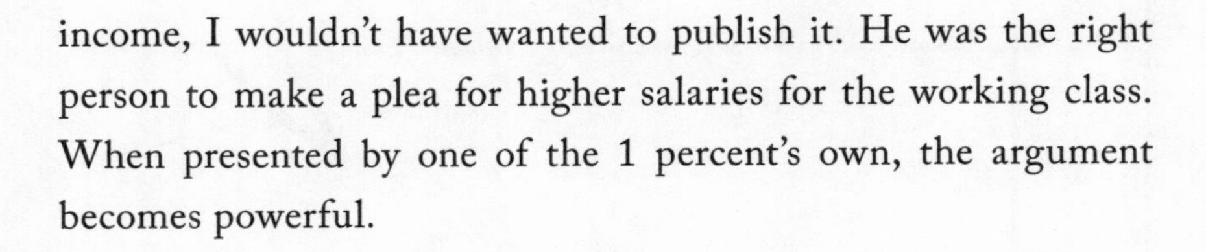

income, I wouldn't have wanted to publish it. He was the right person to make a plea for higher salaries for the working class. When presented by one of the 1 percent's own, the argument becomes powerful.

This was the piece Peter Georgescu originally submitted:

> I have been on an important journey. It all started a couple of years ago. I became worried, worse, obsessed having realized that America is facing a challenge, an existential threat to our current way of life. It wasn't Al Qaeda, or the vicious ISIL or whatever evolving radical group from the Middle East, Africa or Asia. Oh, they could indeed do damage to us, like 9/11 did or worse, but we would cope. We would bounce back. That's part of our character and the strength of our nation. My fear centered about an internal threat from within our homeland. America's number one challenge keeps rising like a monstrous Phoenix. Its most visible manifestation lies in the much talked about inequality of income.

This is the version that better reflected what he knew, published August 7, 2015, in the *New York Times* as "Capitalists, Arise: We Need to Deal With Income Inequality":

> I'm scared. The billionaire hedge funder Paul Tudor Jones is scared. My friend Ken Langone, a founder of the Home Depot, is scared. So are many other chief executives. Not of Al Qaeda, or the vicious Islamic State or some other evolving radical group from the Middle East, Africa or Asia. We are afraid where income inequality will lead.

But don't think that because you grew up in a suburb and have led a seemingly uneventful life that you have nothing to say. Oppression and pain and isolation are not necessary components of successful stories. Your real story is what is needed. Look at the novels of Elizabeth Strout, a bestselling novelist and Pulitzer Prize winner. She delves into the lives of people who seem ordinary. The wisdom and insight come when she gets below that surface. In your life and in your writing, you have to be receptive to what's in front of you.

Woody Allen had a story to tell that no one else could tell, because no one else knew what was in his mind. I published it with great nervousness that some detail might turn out to be factually wrong. Even if it was perfect, I knew the reaction would be one of fury. And it was. Some of that fury came from members of my staff. They couldn't believe I had given space to someone they believed was a child abuser. Only a few people knew what I was working on. I didn't want news of the story to leak. I knew a few younger staffers were irate. But besides being a fan of the concept of innocent until proven guilty, I thought I had a moral obligation to run his article because our publication had given his accuser space to tell her story. In college, at work, in your office, you will probably encounter decisions and opinions you dislike, and you just have to deal with them. I knew what some of the editors were thinking: What about Hitler? Stalin? Mao? Would you have given them space to tell their stories? And you know what? I might have. The *Times* didn't have an Op-Ed page until 1970, so we don't know what the editors of that time would have done if that outlet had existed. But I am convinced that understanding evil is just as important as understanding goodness.

6

When to Go Personal

You've figured out what you want to write about—what you need to say, what will stand out, what you have the authority to tell. Now, how do you present it?

Not every essay needs a personal aspect. Sometimes, though, it makes sense to go personal. Some pieces are more powerful and persuasive when the writer's story is central to the piece.

Angelina Jolie was the perfect example. She used her fame to tell her personal story—not to aggrandize herself, but to help others.

I happened to be working at home on the day her representative called. I liked being alone at home occasionally, reading and editing. Sometimes the office felt like a tight turtleneck. At home I could breathe, space out, daydream.

My deputy, Sewell Chan, emailed me to say that an op-ed submission would be coming from Jolie, and did I want to come into the office and handle it. The *Times* was only 15 minutes by subway from my apartment. I understood why he asked. Even newspaper people who never deal with celebrities and show no signs of being in awe of them might be excited about Jolie. She was one of the biggest stars in the world.

I figured Sewell wanted me to say that I wouldn't come in. And so that's what I did. I knew he would enjoy it. A deputy rarely gets to be in charge, and yet does tons of work. I told him, she's all yours.

Later that day, Jolie delivered a piece not about an upcoming film, but about having her breasts removed after discovering she had a gene that predisposed her to breast cancer.

Her writing brought in millions of views and perhaps changed the way some women looked at being screened for their genetic risk of breast cancer. Maybe some got tested for the BRCA1 gene who otherwise would not have considered it. Maybe her article helped some women live to see their children in their first jobs and their first adult homes. I hope so.

Jolie's piece showed the power of using the personal. If she had simply called for more women to get tested, or had even just written that the gene ran in her family, it wouldn't have been so moving. By writing about her breast amputation, Jolie took the chance that her image would be forever changed. That was a huge gamble. Jolie was putting her financial livelihood at risk. If men would no longer be able to buy into the fantasy of her as a sex goddess because they couldn't help visualizing her breast surgery, would she still be successful?

It's scary for us regular people to put personal stuff out there. Imagine the calculation of cost and benefit it takes for a famous person to do it. Betty Ford, the first lady in the 1970s, was bravely open about her long struggle with alcohol and drugs. The writer Andrew Solomon talked about having depression, as did William Styron.

These well-known people put the health of others above their personal desire for privacy.

The next time Jolie's people got in touch, almost two years later, I was in the office, and so I handled the piece. I worked with Arminka Helic, a British politician and friend of Jolie's. I would have expected one of the most famous women in the world to have a gaggle of public relations consultants, so I was surprised to learn Jolie didn't work that way. For things like this, she depended on Arminka.

There was much debate among the editors over whether we needed another piece, part two in the gutting of a famous woman. I felt we did, because she had already put herself out there with a personal and compelling story, establishing a connection with our readers. I argued that running it wouldn't be simply voyeuristic. The second one wouldn't be as shocking, but any woman in a similar situation wanted to know—what happened next to someone with the genetic risk for breast and ovarian cancer?

In her second story, Jolie wrote about having her ovaries and fallopian tubes removed to further minimize the chance of getting cancer. It was less surprising, the second time, although still moving and personal.

Indeed, it was her story, and only her story.

Some of the most popular pieces we ran were revealing and intimate. Often they had to do with elemental issues of life and death, family relations, addiction, and stress. The writer and neurologist Oliver Sacks documented his discovery that he had terminal cancer and wrote about it in a series for the *Times*; the final story ran just two weeks before he died. If he or Jolie had been reluctant to share personal details, they would have produced weaker pieces that readers most likely would not have remembered. But these writers weren't reticent. They didn't obfuscate; they were direct and unsentimental.

When you decide that your personal details will make the story stronger, whether you're a young man writing about the acne that is tormenting you or an old woman writing about her joyful sense of freedom when a long-loathed husband dies, you have to tell it—even if you're afraid it's trivial or embarrassing or certain to bring out hateful comments online. Best to expect that, and avoid reading comments. And remember that vicious people are responding to the personal details because all people are. You don't always hear from those who were moved to laugh or cry.

For many people, revealing personal information is frightening. They worry it will make them seem weak or detract from what they consider their intellectual or professional achievements. I consult with clients who want help with their op-eds, and recently worked with an accomplished author. When I pushed her to put more personality into her op-ed submission, she was adamant: "I don't do personal," she said. She didn't want to talk about the way her childhood connected to the policy arguments she was making. But that childhood had shaped her views and given her a perspective that others didn't have. Providing those details would have made her article richer. She was hurting her piece by refusing to make herself human to the reader.

I often feel rude pushing writers for personal details, but I'm just trying to make their articles more memorable. Sharing personal information can be tough for journalists because many of them are accustomed to keeping private information out of their work. Writers have to do what is right for them, and when I was working with contributors who were regulars, I usually didn't push.

You will have to figure out how much personal detail you are willing to share. Sometimes I insisted on more details as a condition of publishing an article.

One day I heard from a top literary agent that one of his friends had a story about suicide to tell, and would I be interested. The friend was Will Lippincott, a literary agent who had ended up in a psychiatric hospital. Shortly after being discharged, convinced he would never get better, Will made a plan to die. He went up to his country house to kill himself, but at the last minute aborted his plan. In a different facility, he discovered a treatment called dialectical behavior therapy that changed his life, and he wanted to write about it for the *Times* and, as his agent friend put it, "spread the word."

I was intrigued by that email and eager to read the essay. But when it arrived, I was disappointed. Will was indeed spreading the word about the treatment, but he withheld details of his experience. That was his mistake. Not to be totally callous, which of course good editors must sometimes be, but if he wanted the piece to be published, he had to talk much more about his own trauma and much less about promoting the treatment.

That wasn't just my opinion. Other editors who read his piece had the same reaction, and although their remarks might have seemed insensitive, we were all seeking the same result: the best possible story. Of course it helped that we made our comments to one another in email and, unless one of us messed up, the writer never saw the comments in their raw, brutal form. Typical of the comments was this one: "The suicidal half is way more interesting and compelling than the second half. I think it can be fixed if he adds more personal reflection, and dials down the rah-rah tone." So I had to ask Will to expose himself much more—to describe how he felt, say why he decided to kill himself, and explain why he then decided not to.

This was someone I had never met and probably never would, so it seemed invasive to demand that he tell our readers details that his family might not have known. I felt a little ashamed. Was I being a jerk? Will was well known in the world of book publishing, and putting out all that personal info might be something he just couldn't do. But he did it, and he wrote a powerful article because he felt so driven to introduce others to the treatment that had saved his life.

Many writers make that same mistake, talking more in generalities than in the specifics that would make their stories stronger and give them more persuasive power. A former hedge-fund trader named Sam Polk once sent a draft of an article dealing with his wealth addiction. I liked the idea and thought that it might be a Sunday cover. Sam said he had written two versions, so I asked him to send the longer one as well.

He had a great first sentence: "In my last year on Wall Street my bonus was $3.75 million—and I was angry, resentful." He thought he deserved more. He was envious of his bosses for earning larger bonuses. He wanted more money, he wrote, for the same reason an alcoholic wants a drink: "I was addicted to it."

But the essay went downhill from there. It had too many general statements about addiction and not nearly enough about Sam's life. I needed to understand what in his family dynamic made the accumulation of money so important. I wanted to know more about his father, who Sam believed had transmitted the philosophy that money solves all problems.

Sam was gracious, and eager to tell his story. He revised the article to add the particulars about his own experience, and it became one of our best-read Sunday covers. Because Sam had abused drugs and alcohol, he realized, with the help of a counselor, that his relationship with money was similarly addictive. He wrote that there were no twelve-step programs for money addicts, because our culture lauds the addiction.

Not all personal stories have to be grim, about matters like depression and addiction. Tim Kreider, an essayist and cartoonist who frequently contributes to the *Times*, wrote about his passion for his cat—a piece that was later selected for a book on the best essays of the year. The story could have been silly, but it was profound. (And of course, besides loving the article, I knew that our audience shared my interest in animals. The traffic on good animal stories is always high.)

Tim talked about his relationship with the cat to make larger points about human nature and what it's like to live alone and then with a cat. He was honest and he was funny, and he wasn't embarrassed to be writing about a cat. He talked about how demanding she was, so physically close to him that if a woman came over, the cat would force herself between the two of them. He wrote that one of his girlfriends accused him of being in love with the cat. With his typical deadpan humor, he went on to say, "To be fair, she was a very attractive cat."

Some writers intuitively know that their personal story is the way to go, and they don't have to be pushed. A good editor simply has to get out of the way and not hurt the story. One day we received an op-ed from Mona Simpson, the novelist. It was Simpson's eulogy of her brother, Steve Jobs. They had both been adopted as children and hadn't met until they were adults, but then they became close. All we had to do was quickly fact-check the piece and put it on the web. There is no reason to mess with well-done work just to earn your pay. Simpson detailed her brother's personality through thousands of words that were impossible to stop reading, until she ended it with his final words in this world: "Oh wow. Oh wow. Oh wow."

All of us have stories to tell. The strongest ones, the ones that people will remember, often reveal something almost painfully personal even as they connect to a larger issue or story that feels both universal and urgent. The next time you read a news story that interests you, think about how your story might illuminate it. Has your state just put restrictions on abortions? Did your mother have an abortion after having several children, in a decision that affected your family forever? Tell that story. When you were eighteen, did you have a motorcycle crash that was caused by a pothole? You might write about the country's crumbling infrastructure and the personal and health costs from neglecting our roads. Your story, no matter your age or your level of education, will help readers remember what you have said, and they will be more likely to be persuaded by the policy points you are making.

The details of your life will help make your story moving as well as convincing.

PART III

Winning People Over

7

Know Your Audience

If you want to persuade people to listen to you, you need to listen to them first.

You can't possibly influence them if you don't know how they feel and where they might be vulnerable to change. But as a culture, we are listening challenged. We don't know how to listen, or we're not willing to, or both. It has always been hard to get out of our own obsessions and preoccupations, but it is even harder now, in this age of selfies and Instagram and Facebook, when it's all about me and sculpting the image of my life while paying little attention to yours.

Listening is hard. Tell me that you actively pay attention to people when they talk. I bet you don't. I admit I'm obsessed with this. I'm the annoying person who takes a phone off the dinner table and moves it out of reach. If I run a meeting, I ban laptops. Sure, you might need them to take notes, so exceptions can be made. But I've sat next to people who were "taking notes" and then watched as they stopped listening to the meeting and started checking and answering email. It's like taking a drug into a meeting. Distracting. Your senses are no longer sharp.

If you're focused on creating your own brand, you can't pay attention to your audience. You have to know them, whether you're trying to reach just one person or a large group. You have to know who they are; what they will respond to; what they think about; what their fears and biases are.

Sometimes people appear to be listening, but they are just trying to figure out where to jump in. They are just waiting to talk. I often fail to listen, so I know how hard it is. What about you? Do you let someone finish a sentence? I had to confront my faults as a listener when someone harshly and continually criticized me for interrupting him. I thought that he was just being mean and difficult. But over time, watching myself, I had to admit that I was frequently interrupting. I had lived in New York for years, where many people are quick and aggressive, jumping in and out of conversations. Sometimes it's lively and exciting. But sometimes that speedy conversation leaves out people who are more thoughtful and don't want to fight to be heard.

I tried to change. I worked at it. I beat myself up when I thought I had interrupted—and yet I found it hard to stop. I would obsess about it. And still I interrupted.

Try this experiment. When someone is still talking and you want to finish his sentence, because you're sure you know what he is going to say—don't. Don't finish the sentence. Does it slow things down? Make conversation feel a little boring? Maybe at first. But none of us knows what the other will say. Maybe if you let people finish their sentences, you'll be surprised by what you learn.

Shutting off the conversation in your brain and actually listening takes a lot of effort, and it's an effort that most of us don't want to make. We are flaunting our egos. We are impatient. We are showing

Here are some tips on how to listen:

- Don't shake your head while people talk or express any kind of negativity.
- Don't give advice; that shuts down conversations.
- Don't cut people off in the middle of a sentence. Press your top teeth onto your tongue if that's the only way to keep words from escaping. Don't abruptly change the subject.
- Don't look at your phone while you're talking to someone. Stop the chatter in your brain so you can actually hear. Don't start wondering what you might cook for dinner.
- Think about what the person is saying.
- Use eye contact—but don't stare.
- Make appropriate comments and noises to show you have heard, and encourage the person to go on.

off—jumping in quickly to show how much we know, like doing a cannonball off the high dive. Hey, look at me!

Few people listen well, but it's a central tool in communication.

One day I ran into my friend Bob Morris, a writer, at a cafe and told him what I was working on. He smiled, but sort of enigmatically.

"What? What?" I asked. He told me something I hadn't known—that although he is a writer, he was also studying conflict resolution. The secret to bringing people together, he said, isn't to put forward ideas. It isn't to argue or try to convince them of something. It's to listen and to listen and to listen, and when you see a middle ground—go there!

How do you do that?

Stop the multitasking. Twenty years ago, few of us used that word or thought about that concept, and now it's an ever-present concern. New Yorkers used to make fun of tourists who would stop abruptly and look up at the tall buildings, ruining the flow of foot traffic. Now New Yorkers and tourists alike are looking down at their phones on subway stairs, in the middle of intersections, and while paying for a cup of coffee. Multitasking blocks those around you from doing what they need to do. If you multitask in conversation, the person or people you are talking to will feel that they are unimportant. Recently in a store, as I was explaining to the woman there what I wanted, she briefly answered my question and then started looking at her phone. That didn't make me feel that I should support that store ever again. Looking at the phone, taking a call, texting—it's a way of being judgmental and dismissive, a way of saying, I have something in my life that is much more important than you.

To listen, and hear, we need to be fully present and suspend judgment. It can be hard to listen to people who aren't in whatever group we feel drawn to or attracted to, whether it be tall or short, dark or light, fat or thin, young or old. But if you try to overcome that instinct to judge, you will listen better. If you can't suspend judgment, at least suspend the signs of judgment—the frowns, the looking away. You have to seem like you have an open mind. When you make an effort to be quiet and listen, you'll begin to hear differently. Try to feel the emotions behind the words, and show that you hear and that you understand. Don't disagree. Don't comment. Just listen and make noises here and there to make it clear that you're present. To make the other person feel heard, repeat parts of what they have said, and ask questions so they know you are interested and listening. Not questions that are destined for a yes or no answer or one-word answers—real questions. Don't tell people how to feel, or not feel, or whoever you're talking to will stop talking. Start by giving people a chance to explain their ideas and feelings, and you will seem agreeable and willing to listen. Cut them off, and you will never persuade them of anything.

Initially you might see the need to listen as merely a tactic. But you will soon find that the more you listen, the more genuinely curious you will become. Most people do not feel listened to. Maybe that's why they spend so much time on Twitter and Facebook and Snapchat, desperately searching to fulfill that need we all have. That's why they talk to reporters, and therapists, and comment constantly on the web. They want to be heard.

For a number of years, I was a freelance journalist, and one of my regular duties was writing a weekly column on real estate for *The New York Times*. The work involved meeting someone at home and talking about how they happened to end up there and how they felt about it. That reporting could have taken me an hour or so. But I always spent much more time, sometimes three or four hours, eliciting intimate details of these people's lives that had nothing to do with their real estate situations—parents they were estranged from, jobs they hated, siblings who had drug problems. They had never met me and had no idea how unfortunate it might have been if I had published these intensely personal details. I didn't, mostly because those notes weren't relevant to the story at hand. But I

Here are some ideas on how to interview someone:

- Find out everything you can about the person online.
- Find out everything you can about his employer.
- Think of some questions to ask at the beginning to get it going—neutral ones like "Where did you grow up?" or "Where did you get that great shirt?"
- Think of some questions to ask if things suddenly slow down. These should be provocative and elicit more than yes or no answers.
- Save your most personal or threatening questions for last.

liked stories. Once we had established a rapport, they forgot I was a reporter. I had put people at ease. I had become a friend, and they trusted me.

People are almost always dying to talk, if only people will listen.

Connection is sometimes instant, like a chemical reaction, and effortless. But more often, you need to ask questions, and listen, and show that you're listening so the speaker knows you get it.

It's hard work. I always wanted those real estate interviews to feel like casual conversations between friends, so people would openly share their experiences, but that doesn't mean I didn't prepare.

Before arriving, I learned what I could about the neighborhood and the building, and I made a list of questions that I thought would lead to a friendly conversation and avoid that stilted interview feeling. Simple questions, like "Why did you move here?" But also more complicated ones, like "Is there anything in the apartment that makes you feel especially good, or bad? And why?" I wanted them to feel comfortable talking about how a location influenced their lives and reflected their personalities.

The social value of listening has been well established in academic research. People like people who focus on them and ask questions. In a study published in 2017, Harvard researchers found a consistent relationship between question asking and liking. People who asked more questions were better liked by the people they were talking with, especially if they asked follow-up questions that showed they were listening. Question asking, which shows interest, also led to more dating success in the speed-dating situation that the researchers studied. In one-on-one situations, when two people listen to each other, they become more open to the other's politics and point of view. The personal and political are always melding like that. Long conversations are more likely to show both sides that they are similar in one way or another, and that's when bonding, and agreement, and change begin to occur.

It's interesting to play with the concepts of listening on a personal level. But how do you apply these lessons when you are trying to reach not just one person, but a large audience? It's more difficult, but the same principles apply.

If you are aiming to reach readers of a certain publication—perhaps *The New York Times*, the *Wall Street Journal*, or the *Guardian*—you need to understand who is most likely to read that publication. You must always think about the audience you are trying to reach. You can do that by looking at what is published, at the

What liberals should read and watch to understand the other viewpoint:

- *The Wall Street Journal*
- *The National Review*
- *The Federalist*
- *Drudge*
- *Fox News*

What conservatives should read to understand the other viewpoint:

- *The New Yorker*
- *Slate*
- *The New York Times*
- *Politico*
- *The Washington Post*

kinds of stories that are most popular, at the comments people write. Think about your intended readers, and consider what their biases might be.

You need to listen so you know how to meet objections, and to determine what argument will be most persuasive. To understand the likely biases of your audiences and to craft a strong argument, research other points of view by going to sources you might not regularly read. People get stuck in their reading habits. If they're liberals, they might read the *Times* and *The New Yorker*. If they're conservatives, they might read the *Journal* and the *National Review*. Don't read only websites that confirm what you already believe. Read publications that represent a wide range of views. It's fun and fascinating to compare their world views. It's not a big commitment;

just sign up for the email newsletters. If you are researching a particular issue you want to write about, look at sites with an opposing viewpoint and study their rationale and their evidence. (You might find that you agree with them!)

Then your task is to reevaluate your own claims in light of that research. Doing this can only strengthen your argument. In today's polarized climate, too many people—and this tendency is always on display during political campaigns—believe that anyone who thinks differently from them is stupid or just doesn't know the facts. That's a devastatingly wrong point of view. You have to start by understanding that smart, rational people might disagree with you, and they have good reason to do so. If you disdain the opposition, you will never persuade them of anything. The stereotyping that goes on in the world is breathtaking. As someone who was born in a small town, I become hyperaware when I hear people talk disparagingly of rural people, of Midwesterners, of Southerners, as if those people had no brains. At that point I shut down and stop listening to anything that person says.

It's tough to accept that people might endorse something that seems absurd to you. When Donald Trump was elected president, most people at the *Times* were shocked. Few in the newsroom actually thought it was possible, after the story appeared of Trump boasting of grabbing women's genitals, for a man with that history ever to win, and yet a majority of the white women who voted chose him. When you think something is ridiculous, then it's hard to actually listen, much less to realize that a woman might vote for Trump because she liked other things he had to say.

To reach my readers when I was the editor in charge of Op-Ed, I had to understand what their biases were likely to be. Although I liked finding articles that challenged the liberal readers and made them uncomfortable, whether from the right or the left, I knew that those articles would be useless if they didn't find a way to address people in a way that would make them listen. Writers don't have to agree with their audience, but they must understand what their readers' viewpoints are likely to be.

I remember the day I was hanging around in the office of Frank Bruni, one of our columnists, wondering why so many men who transitioned to be women adopted an extremely feminine style. They seemed to embrace the strictures that women born as women had spent years trying to escape.

"Why do they have to turn into parodies of women?"

Frank laughed. "You have to talk to my friend Elinor," he said. "We just got off the phone and she was saying exactly the same thing."

The minute I started an email conversation with Elinor Burkett, an author and moviemaker who had once collaborated with Frank on a book, I knew she had a point of view I wanted to put out in the world. She agreed to write something, and if it worked out, I thought it would be a good Sunday cover.

I think she understood intuitively how to reach *Times* readers. She knew their likely prejudices. In an article titled "What Makes a Woman?" she started out with a story that was bound to resonate with them. "Do women and men have different brains?" she asked. After raising that question, she went on to recall the case of Lawrence H. Summers, who as the president of Harvard suggested that there were differences in the brains of men and women. He was denounced for being a sexist and for implying that women had lesser brains. Some alumni stopped giving. But then, Burkett went on to ask, why was it okay when Caitlyn Jenner, born Bruce, said pretty much the same thing in an interview with Diane Sawyer? Jenner said during the interview that "My brain is much more female than it is male," which clearly implies a difference.

Liberals who had been so quick to chastise Summers praised Jenner for her bravery. Why? Because Jenner was transgender and liberals supported her, while they were more likely to find fault with a heterosexual man like Summers.

Starting with an apparent shared liberal understanding and then pointing out an example of how it was being contradicted was a smart way to go into a story. The newspaper had run so many editorials in favor of transgender rights that it seemed to be a core value of the readers, or at least of the institution. If Burkett had opened with an attack on the femininity of transgender women, she would have lost readers immediately. The way she structured her piece, she was more likely to carry them along.

That is a classic approach: If you think this, why do you also think something that appears to be the opposite? Pointing out a contradiction might make your audience look at an issue differently. Sometimes showing that you understand your audience is simple. Just start your essay by telling them that you know what sorts of things they worry about, because you worry about the same things. One of my clients, a lawyer, hoped to publish a piece he wrote in the *Times.* Although he is a very good writer, his first sentence was too technical and a bit off-putting for an audience of generalists. Here's what he wrote:

> *Later this month, the U.S. Supreme Court will hear arguments in* United States v. Microsoft, *a long-running dispute between the federal government and technology community over digital privacy.*

I thought he should get to the central point faster and also start with a broad question that would appeal to *Times* readers, who likely were worried about their digital security. So I suggested this:

> *Should the U.S. government be able to look at your emails if they are stored on a server in another country? Or does the government's right to examine digital evidence stop at the U.S. border?*

His piece was accepted and left mostly intact. To me, and apparently to his editor, that approach made sense because it opened with an idea that spoke to a large portion of the audience. Listening to your audience means you have some idea of what people will want to read. If you're writing for different publications, read them carefully to understand their readers and the interests of the editors.

Whether you are addressing a group or an individual, listening is hard. I still catch myself interrupting more often than I would like. But now I understand that I'm getting in my own way, blocking my opportunity to know other people. If you actually listen, you might hear something that will change your life—or at least reveal surprising information that's just fun to know.

At a party, my husband asked a man we had just met about his choice of orange sweater and orange shoes. "Is that a fashion statement?" my husband asked, knowing the man worked in the fashion business. Well, it turned out not to be a fashion statement at all. A thief had recently stolen all of his shoes except the orange pair. A simple question, an astonishing answer.

8

You Like Dogs? So Do I!

In any kind of persuasion, whether it's done in writing or in person, it is essential to establish similarities and shared values. We are persuaded by people we like—not by people we don't. In just about every situation, we're more likely to accept information—any kind of information—when it comes from someone with similar viewpoints.

If you establish commonality and then bring up an issue that might be a source of disagreement, your audience is much more willing to listen because of the connection you have already made. Research by psychologists has confirmed and reconfirmed that phenomenon. By agreeing with your audience, you're much more likely to change their minds, as counterintuitive as that might sound.

And while it might seem obvious that we're similar to our friends, UCLA and Dartmouth researchers have taken that idea beyond the anecdotal. They studied graduate students, asking each of them who their friends were in the program. Using this information the researchers could map out who the students were closest to in their social group and who they were most distant from. Then the researchers asked people to watch a range of videos while having an MRI to measure their neural activity. The study team found that friends have similar neural responses to real-world stimuli. They could predict who people were friends with, and more generally, how many "degrees of separation" people were from one another by looking at how their brains responded to video clips. So we are, on a neurological level, similar to and bonded to our friends. And studies have shown that similarity leads to persuasion. Our minds shape the minds of our friends, and vice versa.

So it's always valuable to make that connection with people, whether you're writing an essay, giving a lecture, or trying to get your neighbor to stop using a noisy leaf blower every Saturday morning. Don't just launch into "the facts" or start with your opinions. Try to establish similarity. It can be about a musician, a TV show, or an animal. "You like dogs? So do I!" And then the pictures come out, and you have established a link. It might seem like stupid small talk, but it's not; it's a way of affirming that you belong to the same group, that you have shared values. You need to consider what they worry about, what they think about, and why they might not be sympathetic to what you have to say. You might be giving a speech to high school students or writing something that you hope to see published in *Foreign Affairs* magazine. In either case, it is worth imagining what the audience likely believes and considers true, so you can start on the same ground.

Your beliefs tell me what group you belong to. If you belong to my group, I am more likely to listen to you. Over my years at the *Times*, people constantly criticized the paper; mostly, I just ignored them. I remember watching my daughter's soccer game and having a mother I barely knew start complaining to me that the paper was pro-war. I just sort of smiled and tried to imagine I was somewhere else. When people criticized coverage, I was generally unmoved. I didn't always disagree, but I couldn't hold myself responsible for everything published by such a big institution.

Even so, when my friend Liza Nelson commented that she was tired of the parochial vision of America presented by the *Times*, I listened. She has been my best friend since we met in nursery school. I know her; I admire her mind and trust her judgment. When she expressed her frustrations with the *Times*, I worried that if the paper wasn't speaking to a liberal Democrat in Georgia, it was in danger of not meeting its aspirations to grow both nationally and internationally. Liza affected the way I thought about the stories I chose in Op-Ed by helping me escape the social circles we all inhabit and reminding me that things might look quite different from the vantage point of a small Southern town.

In this quest for commonality, whether you are writing or speaking, don't hesitate to expose details of your life and ask personal questions. If you let your guard down somewhat and tell people something about yourself—maybe you're having a hard time with your boyfriend, or you're frustrated because you don't like your boss—they will reciprocate. And then you have a connection. That makes people feel safe, and it encourages them to engage. Make them see themselves in you. That's especially important if you're trying to persuade someone to hire you. If you don't open up enough to establish some contact and discover some point of similarity, you will be just another resume.

In trying to win over someone, think about what that person needs. The guy using the leaf blower is just trying to get the job done fast, so your complaints about noise aren't likely to get much sympathy—especially if you're just stretched out by the pool while he is working on his lawn. When you think about it that way, you might even lose the urge to tell him what to do, because once you see it from his perspective, it seems more rational and even unassailable. But if Saturday morning is the only day you have to sleep in because it's the only day you don't have to get up early for work, then tell him that, and make it clear that you'd love to work out something that saves your silence but works into his schedule.

What about a more complicated and polarizing issue, like abortion? Let's say I am in favor of it, and I'm trying to get someone opposed to it to see my point of view. I might start by saying, "I agree with you, the fetus is a human being. Let's just get that off the table. Abortion is taking a life." But what if I then say, "The woman's life takes precedence. It's like war. Some lives take precedence." You're more likely to get the argument moving if you've agreed on some baseline issues and only then try to move it in another direction. If I start by saying that abortion should be legal because it's the woman's right to choose, then I am defining myself as having no common ground with the person or audience I am trying to persuade. In debates, Abraham Lincoln was famous for conceding something as a way of winning an argument. He admitted, for instance, that states had rights—but not the right to allow citizens to enslave people.

By establishing that you agree on something, you make a step forward. If you are trying to win someone over, whether in person or in writing, point to others who are in the same social group as the audience and feel the same way. Present their endorsements. If you are writing an opinion piece, mention those who agree if you think that will resonate with your audience, and mention the opposition of those you expect your audience would dislike. One-on-one persua-

So, how did Abraham Lincoln win an argument?

> In a legal case or a political debate, recalled [fellow attorney] Leonard Swett, Lincoln would concede nonessential points to his opponent, lulling him into a false sense of complacency. "But giving away six points and carrying the seventh he carried his case . . . the whole case hanging on the seventh. . . . Any man who took Lincoln for a simple-minded man would wind up with his back in a ditch."

From *"For a Vast Future Also": Essays from the Journal of the Abraham Lincoln Association*, edited by Thomas F. Schwartz (New York: Fordham University Press, 1999).

sion is as simple as saying to your husband, "I think we should watch *Inspector Morse*; John and Gary like it." If you are in the same social group, and these friends have made good recommendations before, then their influence carries weight when you are trying to persuade someone to do something.

Think about the astonishing rise of the power of "influencers" on social media.

Celebrity endorsements follow the same principle. If you like me, then you will probably like what I like. We trust people who trust us, and we like people who like us. How do you reach that sense of sameness when you are trying to persuade someone? Focus on what you share, find the spot where you connect. When you're

What tricks of persuasion does Jonah Berger use?

Jonah Berger, a professor at the University of Pennsylvania and author of *Contagious: Why Things Catch On* (2013) and *Invisible Influence: The Hidden Forces That Shape Behavior* (2016), likes these tactics the most:

> Mimicking is extremely impactful. When mannerisms, posture, or even the same language is used, mimicry builds trust and rapport and increases persuasion. When someone emails and says, "Hi XX" versus "Hey XX" or "Dear XX," using the same language increases liking and affiliation. Make the desired behavior visible. Show them others are doing it. Enact the behavior you want them to imitate, or show them a high-status or desirable other who is doing it. "Monkey see, monkey do" is a powerful phrase, but the *see* part is really important. The easier something is to see, the easier it is to imitate. So make it visible. Want kids to eat their vegetables? Show them you eat yours. Want people to vote for Democrats? Show them that people they want to look like or affiliate with are doing it.

trying to reach a consensus in person, mirroring is a useful technique. It's a tactic that some family therapists employ. Mimic the other person's body language and speech patterns, and you will increase feelings of similarity and comfort. It may seem creepy, but people like people who remind them of themselves. That's how good salespeople operate.

If you share some priorities and goals, then it's much easier for someone to say yes—and much harder for them to say no. Both sides have an investment in the same thing. The same principles used in one-on-one persuasion can be used in writing. Know what will make your audience feel the need to agree with you. Understand the power of demonstrating similarities. Knowing that you both like dogs, as trivial as it sounds, might be the basis of a powerful connection.

You can use these ideas in something as simple as an email to someone you're hoping to meet. Emphasize what you share. Maybe you both played lacrosse in college; mention that. You are much more likely to get an answer from someone you don't know if you show that you understand something about the person you're addressing—demonstrate that you respect them and that you are similar in some way. Then, and only then, ask for something. If someone asks for something, it's human nature to want to say yes. We do this partly to be nice and partly to avoid confrontation.

Even when we're not being asked for favors, all of us respond to people who like us. We like to be flattered. We like to be praised, and given compliments, and told we are right. Jennifer Chatman, a professor at Berkeley, has found that there's no limit to the amount of flattery people like, as long as it doesn't seem fake. Use it to get what you want. The flattery doesn't even have to be personal. In a 2010 Hong Kong study, students were given a flyer that said they were being contacted because they were fashionable and stylish. Although the students had to know that it was impersonal and that the flyer was asking them to shop at a store, those who received the flyer were more favorably disposed toward that store than those who did not receive it. Make people feel smart with the right amount of flattery, and they are more likely to agree with you on unrelated matters. If you compliment someone on his tie, maybe he will support your plan for a change in company strategy.

Like everyone, I love compliments. I hadn't been in Op-Ed long when I received a letter—not an email, but a letter—from Shmully Hecht, an Orthodox rabbi who advised and cofounded the Jewish society for Yale called Shabtai, which focuses on bringing all kinds of people together. He wanted me to speak at one of their dinners. I had no idea who he was, or what his organization did. Later, when I was more comfortable in the job, I went to many colleges and organizations to talk about how to write op-eds and what we were looking for. But when I got that letter from Shmully, I was new and overwhelmed. I called him anyway. I think I went because I'm always happy to visit New Haven, where I lived in my twenties. More important, Shmully said that my predecessor, David Shipley, had made the trip and that the dinner had been successful. I admired David and figured if he did it, I probably ought to as well. On the way to New Haven, I cursed myself for agreeing to the visit but decided at least I had declined the offer to spend the night, so it wouldn't be endless. To my surprise, the dinner turned out to be fun. Most of the conversation was stimulating, and I was glad to be there.

I learned a few things from that trip.

One, flattery is powerful. Shmully understood that if he made me feel this was something that important editors did, I would be inclined to do it as well. He made it clear that my presence would be helpful to the students, and he understood what I was trying to accomplish in Op-Ed. Flattery has to be focused on something true, and something meaningful to the recipient. If you're trying to persuade an editor to look at your article or your book, show that you are familiar with his body of work. If he has primarily edited political nonfiction, don't ask him if he would like to look at your essay on boxing.

Two, never assume who your "type" is. Shmully, an Orthodox Jew and Chabad rabbi, could not even shake my hand when we met, because he abides by an ancient Jewish tradition that forbids men to touch any women who are not relatives. And yet, he became a friend.

And three, never accept a ride back to the city with someone you've never traveled with. I don't remember the name of the guy who offered me a ride, and I have no desire to learn it; but when I got home, I thought it was a miracle that I'd survived a trip with the world's worst driver.

9

Play on Feelings

One day I got a note from Alex Williams, a Style reporter, saying that his brother-in-law, Paul Kalanithi, had been diagnosed with cancer and wanted to submit an article. I didn't expect much, but I would always read something sent by a colleague. Being polite to your colleagues is always the right thing to do.

When I received the essay, I knew that it was a nearly perfect piece of writing. Kalanithi, a doctor in his mid-thirties, wrote about discovering he had widespread lung cancer; because of his training, he could look at his scans and see that he likely had little time left to live. He was used to looking at images and then having to deliver difficult news to patients—not to looking at images of his own body and seeing that he was dying. I felt stupid writing back that I "really liked" his piece. I don't think I captured my sadness at what he was going through and my admiration for him as a writer.

I made minor edits. Without being maudlin, he used his essay to connect to the universal fear of death and argued that we all need to live fully while we can. Paul was so helpful and calm in the editing and fact-checking, which had to have been difficult when you're about to announce to the world that you have terminal cancer. His piece was exceedingly popular. Before he died, he wrote most of a book about his experience as doctor and patient. The book, *When Breath Becomes Air* (2016), was finished by his wife after his death and became a bestseller.

If you want to be persuasive, you have to connect to your audience emotionally. It doesn't matter whether you're encouraging someone to live fully and find meaning, like Dr. Kalanithi, or selling a service or a point of view on something as mundane as taxes.

Let's say you've done your research. With an understanding of the audience you are trying to reach, you sit down to write what you are sure will be a powerful plea about whatever it is that has moved you—how to deal with the spread of fires on a hotter planet, maybe, or the unfairness of giving athletes preference in college admissions. It's not a personal story; still, you do need to understand how to play to feelings, how to manipulate your audience.

I suppose that sounds crass. But persuasion is manipulation, a basic truth that should not alarm you. If you understand what people love, hate, relish, and fear, you can reach them by stirring up their feelings and then affirming them.

Articles that touch our feelings are often among the most popular on news sites, and they are more often shared on social media. Sometimes those articles connect with some frustration that people experience; other times, they arouse warmth and sentiment.

Just ask the best advertisers. The subway advertising campaign for the restaurant delivery app Seamless is funny, arch, and completely understands the emotions of New Yorkers, who are reading the ads while underground, frustrated with delays and overcrowding, and eager to get home. Among the Seamless taglines: "Wait for a table? You won't even wait for a walk sign," and "Over 8 million people in NYC and we help you avoid them all."

Unabashedly sentimental is the viral ad "Friends Furever," which Google made to market its Android phone. It shows different kinds of animals in unexpected pairings—a dog and an elephant, a baby rhinoceros and a sheep—playing and hanging out together. You remember it and want to share it because it makes you happy and grateful to be alive.

Anger is another powerful feeling that can be tapped. In a *New York Times* essay, the writer Kim Brooks told the story of how she was arrested for endangering her child merely because she left the child in the car while she ran into a store to pick something up. To any woman familiar with the struggle to do a job, take care of children, and make a home, the idea that a woman could be expected to do all three without ever needing to leave her children for even a minute was infuriating.

If you can arouse feelings in a reader or viewer, then you can have influence. Some writers mistakenly crush feelings from their essays in an attempt to be taken seriously. I remember hearing from a writer who was talking about the disrespect bordering on racism that his fellow Germans had shown toward the Greeks, who at that time were suffering from financial problems that threatened to harm the European Union. His pitch for the article was full of passion and feeling, but much of that had disappeared by the time we received his work. We urged him to restore the emotion, and he did, because his feelings about his countrymen were a way of involving us in the argument and making it stand out among the many articles on that crisis.

Feelings do far more than help us engage with articles, speeches, and books. They drive our rational conclusions, in the sense that the conclusions are just an excuse to justify the feelings. Influential research looking at how people make decisions, done by Amos Tversky and Daniel Kahneman, exposed the myth that people make choices in a fully rational way. Many of our financial choices illustrate that, as do our electoral ones. Often in elections, people follow their feelings and only later come up with reasons for their actions and beliefs. As a presidential candidate, Donald Trump masterfully played on people's feelings, on their need to vent their anger over changes in society. Thanks to those feelings, some voters ended up supporting a man whose policies wouldn't benefit them. Trump pushed lots of positive messages—Make America Great Again—but his underlying tactic was to arouse the feelings of people who felt marginalized and bypassed by other races, other countries, and by women, and to affirm the validity of those feelings.

Maybe their desire for a powerful dad and a strong, decisive leader prompted such people to vote for someone who would later do nothing for them. But it wasn't rationality that guided them; it was their feelings. Psychologists call these mental shortcuts heuristics—the rules we use to quickly make decisions, even on complex matters. The trouble is, those heuristics that we use to get through a day also sometimes lead us to do illogical, irrational things.

Sometimes the strong feelings that come through in your piece and create its voice will help you get published because the editor knows that feeling and is moved. I remember getting an article from the travel writer Paul Theroux about the damage done to the American South after U.S. companies abandoned those states for cheaper labor in China. Theroux was upset that the rich chief executives who had approved those moves then wanted to turn around and "help" the poor. I responded to his passion because it lifted his story above others that might have said the same thing in a dry, analytical way.

Emotional stories get the most distribution on social media. Feelings are central to popular entertainment as well. One of my favorite scenes in a television show was in *This Is Us*, which provided a master class on how to play on feelings. The dad, Jack, can't afford the car he wants for his wife and three young children. He asks the salesman if they can talk privately in his office, where Jack proceeds to spin out how he sees his family in the future in that car, how their lives unfold, and packs the story with sentiment and feeling. It's not surprising when the car salesman figures out a way to help Jack. He connected; he feels it; he wants to help. And of course the scene is funny because it reverses the usual practice of the car salesman trying to talk a customer into a car by exploiting his feelings.

Sometimes, you can write in a way that engages feelings even though the words aren't openly emotional. Jerry Saltz, a Pulitzer Prize–winning art critic, wrote an article for *New York* magazine looking back at the time in his life when he worked as an artist, not a critic. I suspect that Saltz, just in writing about how it felt to make art and then give it up, was emotionally reaching the many thousands of young people who arrive in New York determined to be successful in some kind of art form—theater, writing, dancing, painting. He wrote about his feeling of being driven, of being captured by the need to do it, and finally, about being unable to continue. He was blunt and made his feelings of failure clear.

Although you can reach people by arousing feelings of sadness, pain, and sorrow, we are all inherently optimistic, and it is worth remembering that. Our optimism endures even when we encounter facts that would seem to call for reevaluating the situation. In a study led by Tali Sharot at University College London, nineteen volunteers were asked to estimate their chances of experiencing eighty different bad events in the future—things like getting Alzheimer's or being robbed. As the study participants responded to questions, the researchers scanned their brains with an MRI. Afterward, Sharot and her research team showed participants the actual statistical likelihood of bad things happening to them. Then participants were again asked to estimate their likelihood of experiencing those bad events. This time the researchers found that participants tended to revise their estimates to make them more positive when the information pointed that way, but did not make them more negative when the facts clearly suggested that they ought to be. The study participants also overestimated how long they were likely to live. The MRIs showed that their brains simply ignored the bad news. Strikingly, even those who were pessimistic about the world were optimistic about their own lives.

Because most of us are more optimistic than realistic, we tend to underestimate the chances of things like losing our jobs, getting divorced, or being diagnosed with cancer. Being optimistic—or slightly in denial—is an evolutionary advantage. It makes us psychologically able to keep venturing into the world, taking risks, and believing in the future. (But it also makes us a bit stupid about things we ought to do, like saving for retirement and scheduling unpleasant medical tests like colonoscopies.) If you were perpetually worried about dangers and threats, it would be hard to function. The secret is to be alert but not immobilized: all of us can learn from Chekhov's play *The Cherry Orchard*, whose characters are so loath to face reality that they are frozen and must watch passively as their family legacy is lost.

In your persuasive writing, remember that scaring people and being negative does not generally agree with our fundamental natures. We are hardwired for optimism, so we generally respond better to positive messages than negative ones. People didn't stop smoking only because they were scared. They also stopped because quitting became a stylish thing to do, and they wanted to be like their nonsmoking friends.

Shame and fear have too often been the tools of the environmental movement in its efforts to change behavior. Giving people depressing information hasn't worked. It just feels threatening. It is easy to distance yourself from something like that, to push it away and focus on your day-to-day life. The long term is just too abstract. In the book *What We Think About When We Try Not to Think About Global Warming* (2015), the Norwegian psychologist Per Espen Stoknes writes that people don't want to hear repeatedly about doom, particularly when there is no clear enemy. Those who are trying to get action around climate change need to balance threats with solutions and personal messages. People need to hear about steps we can take to deal with the warming world. Other writers have made similar arguments. In one study, several psychologists recruited people online and then asked them to choose between environmentally friendly and environmentally unfriendly options—for example, buying refrigerators that used less energy. As people chose, some saw a sentence on the computer that said, "Keep in mind that you might feel proud about your decisions." Others saw this instead: "Keep in mind that you might feel guilty about your decisions." In most of the scenarios, those who thought about pride, or got the pride reminder, were more likely to choose appliances that helped the environment.

People need to hear something positive. We don't want to feel guilty or hopeless.

In your writing or talking, if you can put people in an optimistic mood, they are more likely to hear you. Fear is strong, but so is hope. Fund-raisers for charities have learned that lesson. Those that emphasize happy transformations—even when raising money for somewhat grim situations—do better. Nike doesn't tell people to exercise because if they don't they will die, but instead uses stories about people who have transformed their lives—amputees running marathons, octogenarians swimming, and the like. When charities offer a sense of hope, donations go up. Books about the Holocaust that are set in the camps don't sell well, while those that show something positive—like a Christian who rescued Jews, as in *The Zookeeper's Wife* (2007) or *Schindler's List* (1982)—appeal to people's desire for a happy ending. Even the devastating story of Anne Frank, one of my favorite books as a child, was rooted in a positive outlook. It was set in the world of her mind, not in a concentration camp.

So, in your writing, understand the human bias in favor of being affirmative and positive. Make more positive statements than negative statements when you are trying to reach people, because they will be more likely to absorb that information. In your efforts to persuade, stay away from depressing images and crying people. It's not effective to shame people, to make them feel guilty, to bait them or make fun of them. We all want inspiration.

10

The Power of Empathy

A car cuts in front of us on the Long Island Expressway.

"I hate these fucking drivers," my husband says.

Traffic is slow. It's hot. We're both squinting into the setting sun, which makes it hard to see. He is stressed, annoyed. I'm annoyed by his stress, and angry that he can't just accept the traffic and relax.

"Why do you care?" I lash out. "You're being stupid. We'll get there in time. What's the difference?"

"Leave me alone!"

If that scenario is familiar, it's because it occurs regularly in couples and families. And if it is familiar, you might know that my behavior in that exchange only made things worse.

If I wanted to persuade my husband to chill out, I should have empathized with his frustration. Said I felt the same way. Instead of fighting his frustration, I could have changed the subject. Found a podcast about politics he would have liked, or at least one that would have offered a different target for frustration. Put on classical music, or maybe one of his obscure favorites like "Jesus' Blood Never Failed

Me Yet," by Gavin Bryars. Anything to take his mind off our inching toward Manhattan, beckoning us but never to be attained.

We all know intuitively that lecturing and hectoring create resistance, not compliance, and years of psychological research back up that instinct. You can't bludgeon people into agreeing with you, or into changing their ways. You can only try to assert influence. Persuading people often means suggesting something in a way that is not an order but almost an invisible suggestion. You don't come around to something unless there is a good reason for you to do it.

When someone is talking about her struggle with weight, you don't say, just stop eating. But you might say, "When my wife was trying to lose weight, she cut out wheat and dairy." It's supportive, perhaps persuasive, but indirect in a good way. You're not saying, "You should do this."

Whether writing or speaking, you have to study who your audience is: understand their age, their education level, their values. Empathy is sensing what others feel. When you understand what they feel, you might intuit how to act on that information.

"The Universal Prayer" by Alexander Pope is often quoted for a reason:

Teach me to feel another's woe,
To hide the fault I see;
That mercy I to others show,
That mercy show to me.

Empathy is not inherently negative or positive; it's a tool. It can be used generously or cynically. Richard Friedman, a psychiatrist and professor at Weill Cornell Medical College and a regular writer for the *Times*, says that many people misunderstand empathy. They think it means to identify with others, to be sympathetic and truly feel their pain. But in reality, empathy involves understanding the psychological makeup of other people. It's about knowing how to get under their skin. Brilliant politicians, demagogues, and psychopaths are often empathetic. (So are the best psychiatrists, and I think Richard is one.) They make their target feel understood, known. Depending on the moral compass of a leader, empathy can be positive or destructive. Either way, it's a connection that lets you get through to people.

I wish I had understood the power of empathy when my older brother, Deke, a Princeton graduate who had a PhD in economics but little patience for the ways of the world, was still alive. We had been close as children; indeed, my first words were, "I go Deke." But in our thirties he pulled away, making it clear he found me annoying and not worth his time. After an early life filled with achievement in academics and sports, he had gradually rejected much of the world, preferring to be with his wife and children, to walk in the woods and keep company with his dogs. Most people seemed to disappoint him, me included. A rupture in our relationship came when, in my early forties, I was carrying out the details of my mother's will and he thought I had been too slow to get the title of her car changed so we could give it to a family friend who needed it.

After that, we seldom spoke. If I was visiting my father, he always called Deke and then quickly passed me the phone. My father wanted to assure we had contact. When he was growing up in Marietta, Ohio, it always upset him that his mother never spoke to her brother—and he lived next door. If I had understood the power of empathy, I might have told my brother, "I am sorry that I seem to be failing you; I am doing my best, please forgive me." I might have been able to reach him if I had made an effort to understand him and change my response to him. If I did, I might have been able to connect. But I never did that, because I was too hurt and angry that the brother I had adored was rejecting me. I focused on my pain, not his. I wouldn't have had to genuinely believe my apology. But if I had done it and given him a chance to be the person to forgive, I might have rebuilt our relationship.

The ability to be empathetic might be an art in decline. Recent studies suggest that both children and young adults are less empathetic than they were a decade ago. Before you go blaming young people, consider the transformation of our culture. The constant flaming and trashing and fighting over social media in forums like Twitter do much to exacerbate the sense that the world is filled with conflict and not compassion. Research has shown that arousing fear diminishes empathy. But even apart from that, just the experience of living digitally seems to reduce the capacity for empathy. When we observe others, our brains activate neurons that allow us to have empathy. When so many people are staring at screens or multitasking, that neural process may be disrupted. The more distracted we become by all the digital possibilities, the harder it is to focus on others and what they are feeling and saying. Attention is scarce, but ever more valuable.

Even if you don't feel sympathy for people who think a certain way, try to understand what motivates them to hold a position. Ask why they feel the way they feel. Understand why they believe something. You want people to feel safe, and you want to minimize hostility. Think about using words that are open, even tentative, in a way that allows the other person to feel empowered. We all need to feel

Richard Friedman, a psychiatrist in New York, suggests using this exercise to increase your capacity for empathy:

- Carefully observe the person you want to communicate with better, and pick out one thing they said or did that you either don't agree with, don't like, or don't understand.
- Now come up with two different explanations of why they might have said or done what they did.
- Ask the person to tell you as much as they can about their experience and do not share your feeling, positive or negative, about what they say. This is about opening your mind to someone else's and learning all that you can about it—without silent or spoken editorial. Get the data and withhold what you think for later.
- Can you now understand better why this person thinks or acts as they do? If not, keep trying, and you'll get it sooner or later.

heard, and if you show respect, your audience will feel that. Christine Comaford, a business coach and serial entrepreneur, advocates using phrases like "What if," "I need your help," and "Would it be helpful if," all of which focus on solutions and take the conversation away from who's up or down, who's right or wrong. Statements like these will encourage feelings of safety, belonging, and mattering.

They also keep you from expressing so much certainty that your audience hardens its views in response. You're trying to convince another person or a group of people that it's fine to accept a different point of view as valid and possibly true. You're not trying to get someone to say, "I was wrong." None of us wants to feel we mistakenly held to a certain belief; pride won't allow that.

But can you teach yourself to be more empathetic, in a way that will improve the quality of your speaking or writing? Perhaps. Start by examining your own rigidity. Sean Blanda, who works for a web startup, plays a game with friends he has christened "Controversial Opinion." During the game, you can't argue—you can only ask questions about why the person feels that way. That kind of practice will hone your capacity for empathy. Being silent and nonjudgmental will help you understand the feelings and fears of your audience, your friends, your spouse.

Once you accept that people on the other side are real people, you also have to accept that you might be wrong and they might be right. As Blanda says, showing empathy can't just be a technique to make a connection so you can get what you want, which is a convert to your side. It's to create the possibility that you might change your mind.

Rapport is a critical tool for people who are trying to get information from terrorists, criminals, and others who don't want to talk. It's not in the target's interest to talk, in many cases, but then somehow there he is, talking. Two British researchers, Emily Alison, a counselor, and Laurence Alison, a professor at the University of Liverpool, listened to hundreds of hours of taped interrogations of suspected terrorists. They looked at what did and did not work, at how the interrogators managed to get the terrorists to share what they knew. One thing was clear: being aggres-

How Sean Blanda plays the empathy game:

In the game "Controversial Opinion," you can't argue, you can only ask questions about why someone feels a certain way. You don't try to win, convince anyone of your viewpoint, or try to score points. When you hear "facts" that don't support your viewpoint, don't think, "That can't be true!" Instead consider, "Hmm, maybe that person is right. I should look into this."

Blanda noticed that when he was with close friends, some people with controversial views would simply not be willing to say them. So the real purpose of the game is to show people that their group is not as homogenous as they think, and to get people feeling comfortable with the idea that they can be in the presence of an idea they dislike. He explained the game in an article on the website Medium that has been read more than 4 million times. Blanda says he thinks that as polarized as people are, they are also realizing they need to change the nature of their interactions.

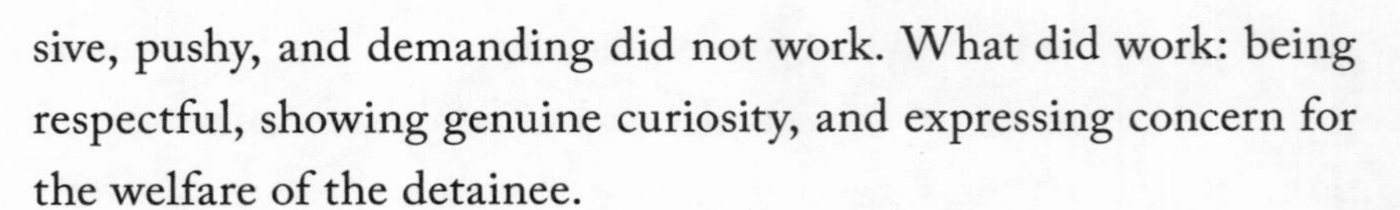

sive, pushy, and demanding did not work. What did work: being respectful, showing genuine curiosity, and expressing concern for the welfare of the detainee.

Once the connection was established, the person wanted to talk, to tell his story, to explain. You have to be nonjudgmental to establish that rapport. You have to lose any desire to dominate and instead, create the feeling that you are in a partnership.

In your writing, never make the audience an adversary. Suspend

Getting a suspected terrorist to talk, from the Alisons' research:

The Alisons found that hostility did not succeed in getting information from suspects; creating rapport did. The following tape, one of many they studied, is of an interviewer meeting with a suspect.

The interviewer began like this: "On the day we arrested you, I believe that you had the intention of killing a British soldier or police officer. I don't know the details of what happened, why you may have felt it needed to happen, or what you wanted to achieve by doing this. Only you know these things. If you are willing, you'll tell me, and if you're not, you won't. I can't force you to tell me—I don't want to force you. I'd like you to help me understand. Would you tell me about what happened?" The interviewer opens up his notebook, and shows the suspect the empty pages. "You see? I don't even have a list of questions."

"That is beautiful," the suspect says. "Because you have treated me with consideration and respect, yes I will tell you now. But only to help you understand what is really happening in this country."

moral judgment. And if you're in a one-on-one situation, it's important to make clear that the other person doesn't owe you anything. The Alisons found that suspects were more likely to open up when the interviewer emphasized their right not to talk.

There's little empathy demonstrated in current political dis-

This dialogue would have worked better with my husband than the one I used:

A car cuts in front of us on the Long Island Expressway.

"I hate these fucking drivers," my husband says.

"I know; it's making me insane. What should we do while we're stuck?"

"I don't know. We're going to be late."

"I'll check the map. Oh you know, we're not going to be late, even with this traffic jam. Let's listen to something. Do you want the radio or a podcast?"

"I wish we still had that comedy show."

"Oh, yeah. We do. I'll find it."

course. It's challenging to find articles that show an understanding of the possible range of emotions and feelings that reasonable people might have. Even Barack Obama, and certainly Martin Luther King, sound quaint when talking about America being for all of us. Tribalism on both the left and right combined with a lack of empathy has become divisive and dangerous.

So don't be a part of that. Don't put pressure on people. If you are writing, demonstrate that you understand your audience, you feel their feelings; and rather than denying them, make those feelings central to your argument.

If you are meeting in person, let the other choose to speak. If you are confrontational or attempt to be controlling, you will only get pushback. A struggle for dominance will never end in persuasion. I have finally learned that lesson.

On car trips, I no longer routinely escalate battles with my husband. Unless I feel like my life is in danger, I try to tamp down my critical, anxious side and ignore his reaction to traffic. I read email or a book until his frustration fades, along with the traffic jam.

11

Don't Argue

I hate political arguments at dinner parties. I used to wonder how I could love ideas and yet detest those endless debates. I remember one in particular, between two of my close friends who took opposite positions on the question of whether it was right or wrong to let people use food stamps to buy soft drinks. One was a passionate advocate for healthy living through his job for the New York City health department. He believed that limiting access to soft drinks by disallowing their purchase with government support was an easy way to improve health and still leave people with plenty of choices. The other friend ran a nonprofit that helped poor people globally. He argued that it was unfair and elitist to decide what people should eat.

I couldn't question the integrity or good will of either of them. But as their voices got louder and they just kept arguing, I retreated, heading to the kitchen to wash dishes. Even by the sink, I could still hear them. They went on for at least 15 minutes, which felt endless to me.

In reality, my guests were both just performing, and they probably didn't expect to change any minds. And in all likelihood, they enjoyed performing, and maybe some others enjoyed watching. In decades of dinner parties and family events, it seems to me that many people, perhaps emboldened by a drink or two, think they can get their way by arguing, by overwhelming their audience.

Actually, it's the reverse. You don't want to go head-on.

Most of the time, if you argue, you will annoy people and make them feel battered and defensive (or worse, bore them). The person you're trying to convince will also argue, voices will get louder, and a standoff will ensue. Ever watch two drivers argue? I'm always worried that physical violence is the next step. Both are trying to be the top dog, and the only way to do that is not to give an inch.

When arguments become intense and anger flares, there is no positive outcome. Before you know it, you're telling your aunt she is a stupid fool, thus removing the chance to make any progress at that moment and probably in the future. Never belittle anyone. That should be obvious, but it's surprisingly hard when you are upset to resist commenting, "You're an idiot." It's satisfying in the moment, but it only increases distance. If you are too intense, you will alienate people. You might trigger an emotional reaction that will shut you out, which is exactly what you don't want. Anger builds anger, in yourself and in others.

I'm not saying that angry polemics have no place in the world of opinion. There is opinion that riles up and stirs up, and there is opinion that hopes to persuade. If you're aiming for the former, go for it; just don't kid yourself that you're bringing anyone around to your side. Argue, of course, if you're in a situation that calls for that: a college debate, a pro and con on a certain subject on a panel. But even in those contexts, you don't want to be argumentative or personal; you just want to be forceful.

Intriguing studies suggest that when faced with aggression,

Suppose you are visiting your mother, and she says, "I just love that Ben Carson." You think Ben Carson, a neurosurgeon who unsuccessfully ran for the Republican nomination for president and then served as HUD secretary in Trump's cabinet, is an idiot. But it's your mother, and you don't think she's an idiot. So, you don't say anything negative. You can only lay the groundwork that will prompt her to think about him the next time he is in the news, maybe even soften her position a bit. Your conversation might go something like this:

"I think he's great," Mother says.

"Well, that's interesting. Tell me what you like about him."

"He's tough. He's an African American who went to Yale and then became a neurosurgeon. That's really impressive," Mother answers.

"Is there something he's done in HUD that you especially like?"

"Well, I don't know, I don't know much of what he's done in HUD," Mother answers.

"He's not a bad guy, but he has never done anything to suggest he can run a housing agency. He even admitted that he thought brain surgery was easier!"

Mother laughs.

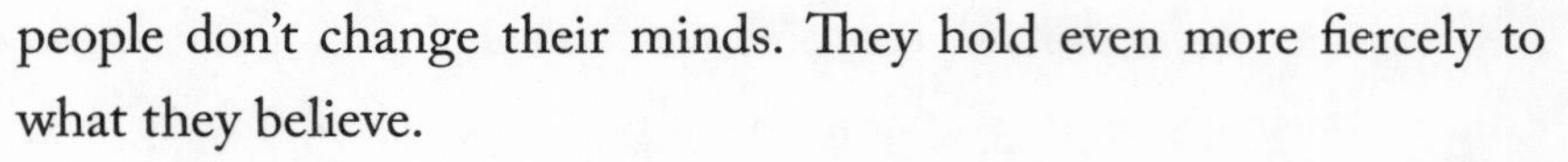

people don't change their minds. They hold even more fiercely to what they believe.

You are probably shaking your head as you read this, thinking of famous columnists or even presidents—Donald Trump—who have successfully taken an argumentative stance toward the world. They prove that anger is a potent emotion to trigger. It can connect you to your audience. It can inject your writing with passion.

But never fight *with* your audience. Anger needs to be a bonding mechanism, not something that creates a wall. Leaders and writers who use anger are speaking to their followers, not attempting to bring others to their side. That's fine. It's just something else—not persuasion. The same holds for those television shows where guys—and it is mostly guys—loudly argue with one another, and people seem to love it. They have lots of viewers. My husband is one of them. For him, those shows are like watching sports, only better. I would never say they aren't entertaining or emotionally satisfying for some people—just that they don't change minds.

We all know what argument looks like in a speech or on television. What is it in writing? To me, it's anytime you make fun of other people. That's a sure way to lose the readers who don't already agree with you. In your writing, don't indulge in personal attacks, guilt trips, or berating. Another form of arguing, even if it's done in a calm voice, involves trying to debunk the ideas your audience believes to be true by battering them with facts that appear to demolish their world view. That won't work. Social science research shows again and again that we are not persuaded by facts, especially when they are presented as part of an argument.

Always concede the good points of the other side. What you want is to be heard, not to win every outing. You want your listeners and readers to be open to a point of view that might be different from what they already believe. So, whether in person, in a tweet, on Facebook, or on the printed page, don't argue. I stop reading if an article assumes something about me based on my gender, geographic location, or income. Generalizing about people is a major way to be hostile in writing. It's aggravating and off-putting when writers take a stance that all poor people are lazy, all white people are bad; all men, predators; and all women, kind and gentle. You get the idea.

The first step is to open up, which is kind of the opposite of arguing.

Show respect for the other person's opinions. Don't put yourself up on a mountain and talk down to people, which is a way of showing disdain and anger. Instead of arguing, look for points of agreement. Let the other person think that all the brilliant ideas belong to him or her. And, as hard as it might be for someone totally convinced of a point of view, show some humility.

Let's say you are writing that New York City should limit car services like Uber. Admit that there's some logic to the argument that people distant from Manhattan might have trouble getting transportation. Admit that you might not have all of the answers. But then, provide the ones that you do have. Express some doubt regarding your own position. Suggest that it might not be 100 percent right. I've seen people kind of collapse in on themselves with relief when they don't feel they have to gear up to fight for each little thing.

At work I managed people for decades and found that in day-to-day life, they always responded well when I was willing to say, "I'm not sure, what do you think?" Don't be dogmatic. Offer choices. Instead of saying, "I want this story to be the cover of this Sunday section," I might say, "I like this story on attention deficit disorder, and I can make it the cover. But it can also hold, so if anyone has something better or more urgent, please let me know." That way you are giving people room to jump into the conversation. You are saying, "I have this plan but it might not be perfect, what do you think?"

People like people who don't try to crush them all the time with their superior knowledge. Showing off that way is just another form of fighting and aggression. If you are too certain, you will come off as smug. If you qualify your statement and say things like, "Well, it is possible that . . . ," you will not seem like a know-it-all who can't be debated. You don't want to create a situation where the conversation is shut down; you want it to continue, for "the other side" to come back with something useful.

Show confidence without being arrogant. People tend to trust scientists, so using the tools of their trade, like charts and graphs, can make you seem more trustworthy. Not all people are alike, of course, but I know I'm influenced by numbers and charts. I have known for years that my cholesterol was a bit high, but it was only when I went to a new doctor who took sixteen vials of blood and produced page after page of charts that I got serious about giving up my chocolate ice cream habit. The swath of red on the chart that signified inflammation was more powerful to me than any single number could be. Whenever I go for chocolate—and of course I still do, just less often—I remember that chart. Sometimes I just walk past the display and out the door. A doctor criticizing me for my choices would never have influenced me. I probably would have rebelled and eaten more. But for me, the visual data was vivid and powerful.

When my friends had that argument about government assistance for healthful choices, I went into the dinner party believing that placing limits on purchases with government money was proper and fair, and there are few public health problems greater than the role of sugar and its contribution to diabetes. I left the party with my mind unchanged.

The dishes, however, were done early.

PART IV

Tips on Writing

12

Tell Stories

As soon as I was old enough to read real books, I found a flashlight and stashed it in my bedroom. While my family slept, I read under the blanket, muting any light that might find its way under the door, often until 3 or 4 in the morning. I knew I would be tired in school, but I couldn't stop. I would read until the flashlight fell out of my hands.

Even now, once I start a novel with a good story, I can't put it down. During the two weeks when I promised myself I would finish this book, after telling myself I wasn't allowed to pick up any novels, I read John Banville's *Ancient Light* and Lee Child's *Killing Floor*. The styles are utterly dissimilar. I was reading for story. I needed to know what would happen. It was hard not to flip to the back. Sometimes I would, just a little, because I wanted to be sure a character I liked wasn't headed for disaster.

All humans like stories. We get sucked in by the characters. Unlike facts, which can be tedious to read, stories are emotional. If you read an analysis about class distinctions, you might struggle through it. But have you watched *Downton Abbey*, a television series about how class is lived? It's fascinating (even if not accurate down to the last detail). I still haven't read a history book about the Nazi occupation of France, but I was hooked by the personal stories in the fictional-but-based-on-reality series *A French Village*. Even knowing the characters weren't real people, I needed to keep watching to find out whether they became collaborators, or fled the country, or blew up their marriages.

Nonfiction persuasive pieces can do the same thing. They can offer characters, suspense, and some kind of satisfying conclusion. I once received an op-ed from a man who had been incarcerated for much of his life. John Thompson wrote about spending eighteen years in prison—fourteen of them on death row—for a robbery and murder he did not commit. Thompson didn't use suspense to build his story; he told us right away that he had been freed from prison after his conviction was overturned. But he presented himself as a character the reader could identify with, mostly by talking about his love for his family. He described how one year, he was scheduled to be executed on May 20 and had come to accept it—until realizing that his final day was just before his son's graduation and the day of his senior class trip.

Suddenly Thompson knew he had to do whatever he could to stop the execution, so his son's experience wouldn't be forever tainted. He begged his lawyers to get the execution delayed. They did get it postponed. More than that, they finally got him exonerated and freed after the courts ruled that prosecutors had covered up evidence that would have cleared him. He had a message and an argument, but he made his point through his story. At the *Times* we received few pieces from prisoners, so they were all special; but none touched me like that. Thompson made a prisoner a real person to me, not a statistic. If he had written a polemic about the risks of wrongly imprisoning people, I doubt that I would have remembered it.

There are classic story forms. I learned one of the simplest and most effective in a television writing course: Get your character up a tree. Then get him down, in 30 minutes. Done.

People are attracted to stories about disaster, about facing adversity and overcoming challenges, about conflict and self-doubt, and about connections made despite some kind of obstacle. Through story, we learn lessons about how to deal with our own lives. All of us have suffered or felt confused. If you start by telling stories that get people engaged, then you can later talk about larger issues and solutions—after, as my teacher said, you get that character down from the tree. Stories draw people in, and they connect brains. Neuroscience has found that when an engrossing story is told, the listener's brain merges with the teller's, and they manifest the same brain-wave action. Stories have been told throughout history as an efficient way to preserve and share information. We remember stories, by and large, better than we recall lists.

When you listen carefully, you're likely to hear stories that you can use in your writing. The Op-Ed department had a party every year, most often near Valentine's Day and usually organized by my old friend Gail Collins, who had become a columnist at the *Times*. It included our regular columnists, writers, editors, and any celebrities who might be entranced by our cerebral crowd and the dour file-cabinet decor of the office. I remember the year that Tom Hanks dropped by, which led to his contributing a charming piece on why he likes typewriters. At one party, the New School philosophy professor Simon Critchley told the story of his disastrous outing wearing a pink shirt, and I begged him to write it for us. He used the story as a reflection on class, clothing, and the nature of swear words.

More recently, I avidly read a story Margaret Renkl wrote for the *Times* about the experience of being loved by a dog. Hardly a novel idea. But she made it concrete and connected it to mothers, to widowhood, to family. By using details like chipped paint to illuminate the intensity of the dog's obsession for its owner, she made the story memorable and the dog a vivid character.

Paul Smith, who trains businesspeople to use stories, sees certain mistakes among those who try but fail to tell stories, and his advice applies to writing as well. Too many people, he says, tell stories that aren't stories—they're not engaging or emotional. They're just plugs for a company's product or way of doing business. Stories have to be narratives about something that happened to someone, with a time, a place, a main character, and some interesting development. More of a problem, Smith says, is that many people don't recognize a good story when they hear one.

Try this experiment, and see if it helps you develop storytelling skills. Before you go to sleep, write down something you saw or heard that day. There's a reason it's still in your mind. Recently I was walking down Eighth Street in New York, nearing a family that had just gotten out of a car and was headed to a restaurant. Three little girls were dressed in identical floral dresses. Suddenly I saw a phone hit the ground. I heard a crack. The mother started screaming at the girl who dropped the phone; she couldn't have been more than four. "Are you out of your mind? What do you think you are doing?" The man she was with admonished her that it was probably an accident.

"No," she screamed, "I saw it. It was deliberate."

The little girl cried and cried in the face of that rage. I kept walking because to stand and watch seemed impolite. But I wanted to know: Why had the mother let such a young child hold a phone? Why was she so angry? Was it the first time that had happened, or the tenth? Or had she just been fighting with her husband about the hours he spent at work—or his failure to find a job? I still see that scene and think it could be the beginning of a story.

That's the jumping-off point for an imagined story. But there are plenty of "real" stories, and you will collect them by listening.

There's nothing new about the value of stories. The need for them is embedded in our biology and never disappears. If you tell stories, you can sometimes change the way someone looks at the world. Researchers have found that many people are reluctant to believe statistics because they associate numbers with the elite. But they believe stories, because stories are real to them. Although it seems counterintuitive, many people believe anecdote and story before they believe facts. British Future, a think tank in England, found that people responded to stories of individual immigrants much more positively than to statistics about immigration issues. They viewed numbers as manipulated and elitist.

The power of story to change minds has been documented in research settings where volunteers watch movies and then assess whether the movies have affected their opinions. In one study, researchers found that viewers who watched *The Rainmaker*, about a lawyer and a paralegal who get together to fight an insurance company that refused coverage for a couple's dying son, became more liberal on health policy. People who watched the conspiracy drama *JFK*, which suggested the government was involved in the president's assassination, felt helpless and had less desire to participate in the political system. Those who watched *The Cider House Rule*s, which showed a compassionate doctor who performed abortions for young women, became more supportive of legal abortion. So movies reach us, as do television shows.

Comedians, because they are some of the best storytellers, are especially influential. In the spring of 2017, when Congress was debating changes to the health-care laws, the comedian Jimmy Kimmel told viewers about his son, who almost died from a heart defect when he was just ten days old. An alert nurse and a speedy surgery saved the baby's life. Kimmel pleaded with politicians to make sure all Americans would have access to the kind of health care that saved his child.

The video of his monologue was shared millions of times; even Obama weighed in on Twitter, applauding Kimmel for defending his health-care act.

Stories make sense not only of the larger world, but also our personal world. The older we get, the more likely we are to create a narrative about the meaning of our lives. How lucky that you lost your job and had to move to California, because if you hadn't, you never would have met the woman you married; how lucky that your house burned down, because it forced you to start over in a new and better place. What can seem traumatic, even disastrous, later becomes part of the story of your life. We don't usually define ourselves by statistics, but by our progression.

In your writing, you don't have to tell long stories. You just have to make your story specific and real. And don't abandon facts; just weave them into your story. The lure of a story will get people to pay attention and painlessly consume the information. The popular TED Talks rely on story. The most successful ones have millions of views because, in a short presentation, the speakers tell a story about their work that differentiates it from what you would find in academic journals. And although those talks are presented from the stage, most of them would work well as pieces of writing, because the same detail that creates power in the speech would make a written work compelling.

Creating Stories in Your Writing

Look for suspense. What is the dilemma? How will it be resolved? It's suspense that keeps us addicted to television shows that go on for many seasons. Create tension in the story by making readers wonder what will happen next.

Create a transformation. When people read or watch a story about someone who changed in a way they would like to emulate, they are more interested in the facts underlying that transformation.

Use images to help your viewers see. Kimmel did this when he described his baby waiting in the hospital for a lifesaving surgery. Our brains react to image and help transport us into the story. The characters and the setting are so real that they become part of your life.

Be logical in telling what happened. Otherwise people will get confused. You want to keep them engaged, not give them a reason to stop reading or watching.

Make sure the end focuses on the message you want your readers to take away. People are most likely to remember the ending, so don't let your tale just trail off.

13

Why Facts Matter, Even When They Don't

If you force me to listen to facts that I don't want to hear, I will probably reject them. If you try to make me look at information about my favorite candidate that seems to contradict previous stances, I'll just let the logical part of my brain go dead and emotions will take over.

Our brains don't like information that contradicts what we believe to be true. We also tend to remember information that matches the biases we already have. You want me to know that Hillary Clinton took millions in campaign donations from the finance industry even while promising to regulate Wall Street? I'll just continue to support her and ignore your facts. You want me to know that Donald Trump hired many immigrants in his own company even as he proposed sharp reductions in immigration? I'll just figure he had a good reason to do what he did.

We have a funny relationship with facts. We are more likely to share made-up stories on social media than stories that are indisputably true. One study by researchers at the Massachusetts Institute of Technology found that false news moves faster on Twitter than true news, because people prefer it and find it more interesting. They found that it took true stories about six times as long as false ones to reach 1,500 people. And this result applied to every subject area, from celebrity gossip to scientific findings.

Our internet free-for-all creates especially troubled times, because we all have megaphones for our ideas, whether real or fabricated. One astonishing incident was the supposed child abuse ring that Hillary Clinton was running out of a pizza parlor in Washington. Articles about the ring began appearing before the presidential election and, although quickly debunked, they continued to spread. Even false tweets by a made-up congressman were posted, claiming that the debunking was a lie. Fake articles linked the child abuse ring to a global pedophilia ring. The story rang very true to Edgar M. Welch, a young father from North Carolina. He drove six hours to the pizza joint, where he fired his assault rifle in an attempt to free the supposedly captive children. The police arrested him. And that—sadly for him—was true, as was the sentence of a four-year jail term.

That incident shows how tough it is to stamp out fake news when the facts align with what some people believe must be true. Some continued to cling to the story about Hillary Clinton's child abuse ring by insisting that the man who had been arrested was actually an actor hired by the "mainstream media"—an insult meant to include newspapers and television stations seen as liberal.

Facts don't change our minds when something seems right. But even though the web has enabled speedy sharing of false stories, lies are not new. When newspapers were thriving, many cities had at least two dailies—New York had many more. With ferocious competition for readers, press lords indulged in what was called yellow journalism, putting out made-up stories to attract readers and make money. Journalism became more respectable in the mid-twentieth century as advertising rather than money from readers became a steady source of revenue. Advertisers didn't want to be associated with risky stories.

I feel like a sucker for only recently understanding that facts are not all they're cracked up to be. Having spent my life gathering and evaluating facts, naturally I believed in the power of, well, truth. The year 2016 did me in, as it did others. After the British voted to leave the European Union and Americans elected Donald Trump president, the Oxford Dictionaries chose *post-truth* as the word of the year for 2016. Both elections had been filled with lies, but the voters didn't seem to care. Sometimes facts even backfired, which wasn't surprising to political scientists and psychologists who have studied this phenomenon. They know that we don't respond as expected to when confronted with facts; and often, when someone challenges our views by pointing out errors, we not only don't listen, we cling more strongly to the views we have.

As a journalist who came of age in the 1970s, with the inspiration of Woodward and Bernstein finding the truth and bringing down a president who had lied, I had a passion for facts and never wanted to make a mistake. Mistakes seemed so permanent. Once I wrote a story and it went into print, that was that. It would be there forever, in the library in a bound volume for people to read for years. There was no going back and fixing it. I also worked for places that stressed the importance of facts. Most of my friends who were reporters at the *Wall Street Journal* were terrified of ever having corrections, because if you had too many you would be quietly let go. The *Times* was a bit looser; it didn't routinely fire people for having too many corrections, but corrections were a public humiliation.

In 2008 it turned out that the writer of a book who had been profiled in one of the sections I supervised was a fabricator. I was devastated and asked my boss if he wanted me to resign. I think he thought I was crazy. Many others, including all the reviewers of the book as well as the woman's publisher, had been taken in by her stories. But that's how deeply I have always felt the need to publish bulletproof facts. I never lost my terror of making mistakes, which I think was a good thing.

But even I have had to give a little. As digital journalism spread and pushed out print, and publications had to post continuously and quickly, it became clear that a rigid approach to every detail would hinder journalism's survival. There were more mistakes; and although on the best sites they were corrected, people were forced to accept that journalism was not only the first draft of history, but a rough draft. Accuracy still matters to serious journalists, but no editor anywhere can be both speedy and perfectly accurate, so something has to give. Just as digital technology changed journalism, it transformed the culture. All of us have become journalists, in a sense—we share our truths on social media and style our food, our gardens, and our children for photographs on Instagram. Even when I'm just posting a picture of my white dahlia, I move the vase just so, to get the best angle and block out any distracting background. We all have audiences, and we are all publishing for them.

But we are presenting the truth of our lives in only the most limited way. We are showing a partial truth. It's not that facts never matter; they do, when a jury, for instance, finds that someone violated the law and will go to jail for some number of years. But that truth coexists with a larger, more complex social "truth." Our social truth is woven of lies—like the guy who can hardly stand his wife but keeps posting tributes to her on Facebook, presenting the image of a contented couple. Social media propels a personal definition of truth, so that now some people think that if they believe something could be true or ought to be true, it is.

Some people say we're living in an atypical era when feelings are more potent than facts, but that's a misunderstanding of how our brains function. Facts are always less important than feelings. What's new is not our relationship with facts, but our ability to spew falsehoods to a bigger audience than just our neighbors. For decades, academics have shown our ability to disregard facts in coming to our conclusions. If we believe, for instance, that immigrants are more likely to commit crimes, every instance of such a crime solidifies our opinion. In case after case, media and politicians give outsized attention to crimes committed by immigrants: a recent event involved the murder of a college student in Iowa, allegedly by an immigrant from Mexico. The murder fits into the narrative of people who believe that immigrants, particularly those from Mexico and Central America, are a problem, and it will not matter how many times the public is told that immigrants do not commit more crimes than the native-born. When Mexicans are labeled as rapists, that notion sticks—even though their jobs in the United States, and their arrest records, more accurately indicate they should be called farmers.

It's not realistic to think that if only people knew the truth, they would do the right thing. Although democracy rests on the idea that well-informed people will do a better job with government, and that knowledge and information lead to smarter decisions, educated people are no more likely than uneducated people to let facts influence them. Whether we're liberals or conservatives or something else altogether, we go to great lengths to defend what we believe in by fending off the facts that challenge it. In numerous studies, researchers have presented study participants with accurate information on emotionally charged issues like stem cell research, tax reform, and the war in Iraq. They find that when those corrections go against what people already believe, they tend to have even more faith in erroneous facts. Essentially, corrections backfired and did not "cure" misinformation, because people want to protect their beliefs from facts that might do them harm.

People don't like to admit they're wrong. It's a defense mechanism. It's threatening to acknowledge that we believed something that is actually false. So we resolve that problem by clinging to our beliefs and ignoring the facts. We go out of our way to avoid facts that might put us in that uncomfortable situation. We read and watch information that supports our beliefs. It's easy to be wrong about lots of things—like the idea that Barack Obama was not born in the United States, even though his birth certificate shows that he was. But if you don't like the idea that a man with a name like Obama is president, then you find a way to ignore the facts of that case, and you will find plenty of other people online who will support your position by arguing that the birth certificate is phony. Since in theory anything can be phony, or made to seem phony through digital manipulation, each of us can cling to our own personal truth.

How could we as a species have made so much progress, evolving from hunters and gatherers to beings that can create computers and robots, when we are capable of ignoring obvious truths? Scientists believe that this tendency has a benefit and an evolutionary purpose. In *The Knowledge Illusion: Why We Never Think Alone* (2017), Philip

Fernbach and Steven Sloman point out that individually, we all—well, most of us—know little. We depend on the knowledge of others to get through life. I don't have to know anything about climate science to conclude that the planet is in danger, because I'm relying on information gathered by—or even just repeated by—those I trust.

This information-sharing process is efficient. I can save time by relying on information obtained by others, whether it's true or false. That way each of us can specialize in what we do best, and thus the whole society progresses. Besides, we're all naturally a little lazy and prefer to make decisions using as little information as possible. Most people don't want to dig and dig and dig, ask around, read more. We want things to be simpler than that. We like an easy answer, and it doesn't matter if that answer is based on a distortion.

Sometimes this refusal to acknowledge the validity of research and the unwillingness to personally evaluate evidence can have dangerous consequences, as when people decide not to vaccinate their children against diseases like measles. The concept of vaccines is scary, and there's no reason to belittle the fear; you're going to give me a bit of a deadly disease, and I'm supposed to think that's just fine? In rare cases, vaccines do have side effects. People have feared them going back to the arrival of the smallpox vaccination in the 1800s in England and the United States. But without vaccinations, smallpox wouldn't have been eradicated in those countries.

Our biological wiring also allows fake statistics to become embedded in our brains. The more we hear something, the more likely we are to believe it is true. And that belief has consequences in the world. Thanks to our fear of terrorism, we have as a nation spent more than $2 trillion on wars in the Middle East. But we have done nothing against Saudi Arabia, the country of origin of many of the terrorists who attacked the United States on September 11, 2001. We wanted action; we wanted it emotionally; but because we weren't going to attack an ally, we had to attack someone, and the facts didn't matter.

Americans are much more afraid of terrorism than we are of car accidents, even though car accidents are far, far more likely to kill us. And I say that as someone who was anxious after the 9/11 attacks. I was nervous on the subway. I was afraid the city would be attacked again. That fear wasn't irrational; we had been attacked, and it made sense to be afraid of more. But the society-wide fear made the facts about who had carried out the attack somehow irrelevant and spawned a paramilitary society with a permanent army at perpetual war.

Our misplaced fears are intensified because politicians and media focus on the aberrant—it is, after all, more exciting—and so people fear the unusual to an extent that's way out of proportion to the actual danger. Once you scare people, that scary thought will more easily come to mind. When we hear about a frightening event, our animal, emotional brains exaggerate its likelihood. The fear strengthens the memories, and so we overestimate the odds of unusual things and underestimate the odds of day-to-day risks.

Just hearing something again and again makes it lodge in your brain. When that happens, the idea is tough to shake. The Berkeley linguist George Lakoff explains that repetition activates the same neural structures repeatedly, and the more a neural structure is activated, the stronger it gets. By joining fear and repetition, it's possible to string words together in such a way that they become linked in our brains, and it is tough to unlink them—as in "Crooked Hillary" or "radical Islamic terrorists." Those who find a way to embed false ideas are smart because those opinions are represented in the brain by strong neural circuitry and are not likely to change easily, even when people are faced with evidence that their initial stance was based on faulty data.

Does this discussion leave you morose, suspecting that facts are never influential? If so, hold on. There are countless examples of the effectiveness of truth, whether in the hands of amateurs or professionals. Sometimes, "true" facts do become embedded in our brains, and sometimes "true" facts do displace false notions. One of my favorite stories of fact winning out over fiction involves the experience of some high school students in Pittsburg, Kansas, who dug into the academic and professional history of their new high school principal. They discovered that she had gotten her master's and doctorate at a private college that was just a place to buy degrees. They published their story, and the principal resigned. The facts were irrefutable, and they won the day.

In your efforts to write something memorable and persuasive, look for surprising facts. Even one simple fact can be used to startle audiences and get many readers, as *Fast Company* did with a brief article explaining that the richest 1 percent of people on earth control more than half the wealth.

Facts can also alter behavior. Millions of people in the last forty years have started exercising and stopped smoking. Millions have started eating fresh green vegetables and stopped drinking sugary sodas. Soft drinks, a concentrated and regular source of sugar for many people, have been falling in popularity for more than a decade, so the information is sinking in.

But while facts can change behavior, they don't usually change it on their own. They have to be paired with peer pressure, social norms, and emotional appeals. People see what they drink as a definer of their tribe and expression of their values. So now, rather than carrying cola in a plastic bottle, they might choose to carry a BPA-free water bottle. I grew up drinking diet sodas, and now I wouldn't dream of having one. I think artificial sweeteners are bad for me; others might disagree, but that's the fact I'm clinging to, and the one that changed my behavior.

Surprising facts can change minds, if they are surprising to the person who is hearing them. In a *Times* op-ed in 2018, as the battle over immigrant rights became more intense near the midterm congressional elections, Debbie Weingarten wrote that the U.S. government had denied the passport applications of her young children. She said they had been born at home in Arizona, delivered by a midwife. The government, apparently worrying that midwife births were just a way to forge documents for people born in Mexico, had refused to send the passports unless the parents sent more evidence of their citizenship.

That essay shocked me because I hadn't heard about the discrimination against citizens delivered by midwives.

The writer said that in states bordering Mexico, the government was denying thousands of passport applications for children whose birth certificates stated they had been delivered by midwives in their homes. Would the children's passports have been denied if their last name hadn't been Hispanic?

There might have been news stories about this practice, there even might have been dozens; but it was new to me. I don't know how this information will affect me going forward. But sometimes a fact can lodge in the brain and influence behavior for decades. An editor friend of mine remembers a long-ago article in *The New Yorker* by Michael Kinsley that changed the way he thought about polling. In the piece, Kinsley wrote about a poll that asked people whether they thought the United States was spending too much, too little, or just the right amount on foreign aid. The poll also asked them what they thought the government was spending. Most thought the government was spending far more than it actually was. That article, my friend said, showed him that there's little value in asking people questions regarding matters they know nothing about, unless you're trying to determine their level of knowledge. Because of that article, whenever someone proposes a poll as part of an article, he considers whether the people being surveyed will be responding out of ignorance. If they will be, he more often than not nixes the poll. Why ask people questions about something they know nothing about?

Your writing can influence people in a similar way if you do research that uncovers surprising facts—facts that will make your reader think, "Wow, there might be something here." Don't just say that it would be great to make politicians in the United States responsible for their actions. Dig around. Maybe you need some interesting details and facts from other countries that would help you suggest a different route here. For instance, politicians in Singapore get bonuses—or not—based on how well the economy performs.

Investigate the facts that underlie various points of view. If you research the opposition, you will be familiar with the evidence used to make that case. Find flaws in that evidence. This is where facts matter. You can find chinks in the opposition's evidence. Think about how students on debate teams prepare. They don't know until the last minute which side they will take, so they have to understand the claims supporting each side. Let's say you are preparing to debate whether we should increase U.S. military force against Syria. There is a pro and a con to that question, and you can study each side in preparing your argument. Don't assume that you understand the other point of view; you probably don't.

Once you understand both sides, dive in and present your side, reaching the person with both emotional and factual arguments. When you have good evidence, it's a lot easier to counter other people's claims while supporting your own. Don't repeat their falsehoods, because you don't want to give them even more air time and allow them to strengthen their hold on your audience. Reframe the argument.

Even though facts have their limits, your facts must be right. Many people insist that the lies put out by Donald Trump prove that you can "get away" with lies indefinitely. But he is only persuading those who already agree with him. And people who grow to see that he is lying tend to become more critical of him and less likely to give him the benefit of the doubt. If your facts are wrong, you will turn off anyone who knows the subject you are writing or talking about. If you assert that more than half of the schoolchildren in the United States are reading below grade level, and one of your readers in the education field knows that the true number is closer to a third, you have lost a potentially influential reader right there. Because of that error, that reader will not believe anything else you have to say.

One of my most important jobs as the leader of the *Times* Op-Ed department was to assure that facts were checked. It surprised me to learn that the same set of facts could be used to reach opposite conclusions. A conservative and a liberal could use the same facts to make contrasting arguments. And that's fine. But the facts did not change—only the perspective on them was different.

Some of my favorite people over the years I worked in journalism have been fact-checkers. Many of them move on to write novels or become editors; but when they are fact-checkers, they develop a rigorous approach to each word that is worth emulating if you want your facts to stand up under scrutiny. Fact-checkers look at words in a particular way. They aren't, at least generally, worried about how a sentence sounds. They are obsessed with meaning and accuracy. At the *Times*, the magazine and Op-Ed were the heaviest users of full-time fact-checkers, because those departments used so many outside writers.

Use the techniques of fact-checkers. When you check your work, underline or put a check mark by each word or phrase as you confirm that it is correct. That way you won't miss anything. You'd be surprised how many times you can look at a name, be convinced that it is spelled correctly, and turn out to be wrong.

Minimize your mistakes, and you will bolster your own credibility. Which is weird, I admit, given that academics have consistently found that people don't hear facts the way you might think they do. But they still get annoyed when they know something is not true.

Part of using facts well is to respect them. Don't use possibly false anecdotes to make your point. Don't cherry-pick evidence. Understand that some of your readers will catch you out if you do. With all the iffy sources out there and the ability of the internet to spread lies and dubious claims, it can be challenging to be sure of your facts. In the next section you will find a list of guidelines for fact-checking, partly based on a list with examples prepared by Kevin McCarthy and Gita Daneshjoo, two of the fact-checking editors in Op-Ed when I was there.

Tips for Researching and Fact-Checking

Always look for reliable sources. We've all fallen victim to simple untruths that are relatively easy to check. At the *Times*, we did not even consider Wikipedia a source that could be trusted, even though it is worth starting there and using the footnotes as a point of departure. Here is a correction in the *Times* of a story with a small erroneous detail that led to an entertaining correction.

> *CORRECTION: An Op-Ed essay on Monday described bald eagles and ospreys incorrectly. They eat fish, and their poop is white; they do not eat berries and excrete purple feces. (Other birds, like American robins, Eurasian starlings and cedar waxwings, do.)*

Look for several sources of each critical fact, not just one. You're not guaranteed that something is true if you find it in a lot of places, but if you do and they tend to be credible sources, the information is more likely to be true.

> *CORRECTION: An Op-Ed article on Sunday about Arizona and immigration mistakenly suggested that javelinas are pigs. They are peccaries.*

Look out for typos, transposed numbers, and mathematical errors. This is especially important in an argument that relies on numbers. A math mistake can bring you down in the eyes of the editor or professor who is reviewing your piece. Do not combine details from various scenarios to make one point, because you then risk inserting errors like this one that appeared in the *Times*:

> *While the writer did fly economy class from New York to Miami recently (on Delta), he was offered a cranberry-almond bar, not a Luna bar—nor blue potato chips and popcorn (which he was offered on a JetBlue flight to Mexico). In addition, the writer observed flight attendants distributing amenity kits to first- and business-class passengers on an American Airlines trans-Atlantic flight, not the flight to Miami.*

Avoid random blogs, and rely as much as possible on academic research and government reports by nonpartisan research arms. Look at specialized sources, not just the first page that comes up in a search. Journalists pay to use LexisNexis, but anyone can use Google Scholar. You will get surprisingly different results. Do a search on Google of "persuasion and how best to change people's minds," and your first two results are a story from the *Washington Post* and one from *Psychology Today*. They are helpful—but Google Scholar looks in a different universe and presents you with an excerpt from a book by Howard Gardner and an article from the *Journal of Consumer Research*. Also look in Google Books, which will give you access to parts of books that might be relevant to your work.

If there's an interesting fact sourced to an academic article, read the article, not just the summary. Or interview the author. That way you will protect yourself from misinterpreting something critical in the study that might be the basis for your argument.

> *CORRECTION: An opinion essay on May 13 about ethics and capitalism misstated the findings of a 2010 study on psychopathy in corporations. The study found that 4 percent of a sample of 203 corporate professionals met a clinical threshold for being described as psychopaths, not that 10 percent of people who work on Wall Street are clinical psychopaths. In addition, the study, in the journal* Behavioral Sciences and the Law, *was not based on a representative sample; the authors of the study say that the 4 percent figure cannot be generalized to the larger population of corporate managers and executives.*

If someone has a financial interest in something, be dubious.

If something sounds like it can't possibly be true, be suspicious.

Aggressively question facts you agree with, not the ones that go against your biases. You are more likely to believe what you already agree with. Distrust your tendency to believe people who are "on your side," and look for facts from a variety of sources.

Use stories to enliven your writing, but be wary of generalizing from one fact. Remember that the story of one person—an anecdote about, say, a woman who could not get an abortion because of protesters outside of a clinic—is just one fact. Ideally, you will take data from peer-reviewed studies that looked at large numbers of people. Look for consensus among the experts in a field. If most of them agree on something, the odds are you can use that fact.

Remember that we human beings are contradictory. We like to share stories of dubious accuracy, but we also love catching people out when they get something wrong. Be careful, too, in your headlines and the other text you use to sell your argument. Some people clearly don't care much about accuracy, but studies show that you can hurt your reputation by distorting the truth and trying to manipulate people. So in your search for facts, avoid misleading headlines and the understandable impulse to go for clicks and only clicks. People don't like to be fooled. Ultimately it doesn't pay to use little white lies.

Eventually facts can have an effect, but it often happens after the fact. Americans continued to believe that Iraq had weapons of mass destruction even after that was proven wrong. They wanted to believe their president. Over time they began to doubt the story of the weapons, but they found other reasons to justify their country's presence in Iraq, or they simply decided to oppose the war.

When the emotional power of something fades a little, people are more likely to be open to a different reality. But that takes time. Meanwhile, be sure you are the one who is writing with passion, power, and facts that no one can dispute.

14

Focus. Be Specific. Prune. And Kill the Jargon.

I've been reading the Roman orator and politician Cicero, and although I studied Latin for years, I had forgotten how lovely and clear his language is. I could give many examples, but here is a paragraph so filled with insight that reading it and rereading it would be worth your time:

> *Six mistakes mankind keeps making century after century: Believing that personal gain is made by crushing others; Worrying about things that cannot be changed or corrected; Insisting that a thing is impossible because we cannot accomplish it; Refusing to set aside trivial preferences; Neglecting development and refinement of the mind; Attempting to compel others to believe and live as we do.*

It's not the old guys who wrote garbled, tangled-up sentences; it's the new ones. There are philosophers who have taken a hundred pages to make the points that Cicero made in a paragraph.

Simplicity is deceptive. It looks easy. Sometimes I think we all just know too much, and we try to show off to the reader. But instead of attracting attention, the result is often the opposite.

Maybe that's why people avoid short sentences. They worry that if their sentences are simple, it will look like they didn't work hard enough or that their thoughts aren't deep enough. But that's not the case. Crafting simple sentences is tough. Ideas have to be crystallized. Sometimes, complex sentences are just evidence that the writer doesn't understand the subject well enough to explain it. Other times, the writer is convinced that sentences with long words will make him look smart—an idea that Professor Daniel Oppenheimer charmingly debunked in an article titled, "Consequences of Erudite Vernacular Utilized Irrespective of Necessity: Problems with Using Long Words Needlessly."

Most writing is too wordy. Most articles are too long—unless they're not long enough. That's the dirty little secret of all this agonizing among media types about how many words people are willing to read, how much attention they will pay and for how long. At the *Times*, that conversation has been going on for decades. There's one big problem with saying how long or how short articles should be: it just depends. You know how long you can keep readers? Until they're bored. Sometimes they're bored before the end of the first sentence. Sometimes they read three thousand words and wish there were more. It's all about pulling along your readers. If you're not telling a story with all the classic ingredients that hold people: love, war, sex, conflict, tragedy—then keep it short. Make sure each word helps the sentence and moves the idea forward.

Here's a sample of wordy writing:

> The small flames sparked in Northern California prove volatile and unpredictable as they continue to develop into monstrous conflagrations. After a major wildfire, the disastrous consequences cause great disturbances in the humanitarian supply chain, but companies like Brand X strive to restore that disruption and provide an efficient chain of command. While cargo ships, trucks, and planes transport food and water to areas of disaster, sites of distribution are set up to mitigate chaos and competition for supplies. Promoting the fire relief efforts even further, Brand X identifies the unique needs of each individual and provides customary medicinal aid amongst families threatened by the fire.

(From a freelance, unpublished submission to Longneck & Thunderfoot, a digital marketing company headquartered in New York.)

Here it is after being simplified:

> In California, where small fires can quickly grow and become out of control, it is tough to get the necessary help to people where and when they need it. Brand X software helps create an efficient communication system so that the help goes where it is needed, on time.

These are the four most common mistakes I see when I am editing:

- People try to cover too much ground in short pieces, and their writing ends up being too general and sweeping. It is so comprehensive that it says nothing. So: Focus on one or two big ideas and get to your point quickly.
- They write in generalities that end up numbing the reader. So: Be specific. Use details that illuminate.
- They write complicated sentences that are hard to follow, or they just go on and on. So: Prune!
- Finally, people use so much jargon that their work is unintelligible to anyone outside their field. Not matter how complex, ideas can be made coherent to the general reader. So: Kill the jargon.

Readers tend to have short attention spans. We aren't able to take in multiple points simultaneously. When a lot of information is thrown at us, with little air and space between thoughts, we have trouble assessing it. In op-ed pieces, it's best to write about just one or two things and dig into them. When you have strong feelings about something—say, how to make renewable energy profitable—you'll probably be tempted to write a sweeping piece that demonstrates the breadth of your knowledge. But if you're trying to persuade someone of something, you'll do better focusing on one aspect that might be surprising to the reader, perhaps that California already gets more than 30 percent of its power from renewable energy. Maybe you can write about whether other states can use the same tactics—or maybe your conclusion is that they cannot, and California is unusual in this way.

Use your knowledge as a foundation for your specific points. I recently edited an op-ed for a client who hoped to see his work in a publication with a national audience. I thought the writer had tossed too many thoughts into the first paragraph, taking way too long to get to his smart and surprising point: that the "old" media companies should be allowed to band together to make demands of the social media platforms without risking antitrust consequences.

I suggested that he get to the point faster. With a new first paragraph explaining that social media gets the advertising benefit of news content but bears none of the cost of producing it, he could move to the main point quickly.

Next, consider the importance of being specific. It is vital to be concrete, to come up with memorable images. When you give specifics in your writing, you will allow your readers to experience what you are writing about. When I was a young stringer for the Associated Press while a student at Berkeley, I covered a lot of news. I ran to a pay phone and called in whatever was happening that day, which usually included police, students, and tear gas. But once I wrote a feature story for the AP about D'Army Bailey, a new, radical member of the Berkeley City Council. After I turned in my piece, the editor asked for more color. Being a news reporter and young, I didn't know what that meant. I do remember I rewrote the lead to say, "From a pea green office in Berkeley." I took the request literally and added color. Not the worst idea, but probably not the kind of detail the editor had in mind.

Far more memorable was the detail that *Times* critic Dwight Garner used in his review of Bob Woodward's book about the Trump White House:

We knew things were bad. Woodward is here, like a state trooper knocking on the door at 3 a.m., to update the sorry details.

That image of the trooper elevates Garner's review, making it visual and vivid by referencing an experience we all emotionally relate to.

The power of detail paired with simple language was illustrated by a series of widely shared tweets in 2016 by twenty-two-year-old Nafisa Rawji. In her series, she took on the question of sex and consent by comparing it to something we all understand: money and robbery.

Here are a few of her tweets:

If you ask me for $5, and I'm too drunk to say yes or no, it's not okay to then go take $5 out of my purse.

If I let YOU borrow $5, that doesn't give the right for your FRIEND to take $5 out of my purse. "But you gave him some, why can't I?"

If you steal $5 and I can't prove it in court, that does NOT mean you didn't steal $5. Just because I gave you $5 in the past, doesn't mean I have to give you $5 in the future.

And to think a man said "Well she sat on his lap & went to his house." Okay, if I ask you to hold my purse, does that mean you can take $?

By using the analogy of a purse and money, Rawji helped her audience see the question of consent in a new way. If she had just said that

Here's a sample in need of pruning:

> In an announcement yesterday, the company said that it would terminate 100 people in order to maximize profits from its expansion into the packaged snacks business. It is reducing its footprint in the drinks industry as that proves to be less profitable than in the past.

Here it is after the edit:

> The company said it fired 100 people because it was focusing on snacks rather than its less-profitable soda business.

sex without consent is rape, her tweets would have been lost in hordes of others. By coming up with a specific way to portray the experience, she got attention and probably managed to persuade at least a few people to look at the issue of consent in a more nuanced way.

She also made her point with few words. None were extraneous. She didn't write any longer than she had to write—helped along by Twitter's word limit.

In whatever forum, write to the appropriate length. If a teacher asks you to write ten pages on the history of Greeks in America, write ten pages. If an editor says she doesn't want to see more than eight hundred words on how Brexit will be managed, don't turn in four thousand words and say, "Well, I know it's a little long, but I was hoping you could cut." Believe me, I've gotten notes like that, and without even considering what I might be missing, I tap the

While there has been a move toward simple language in legal documents, they are still daunting. Most of us toss aside warranties, insurance policies, even legal documents without reading them. Look at this warranty for my stove and tell me I won't have to call a human being to find out what is covered:

> This warranty does not cover any parts or labor to correct any defect caused by negligence, accident or improper use, maintenance, installation, service or repair. Some states do not allow the exclusion or limitation of incidental or consequential damages, so the above limitation or exclusion may not apply to you. This warranty gives you specific legal rights and you may also have other legal rights that vary from state to state.

Delete key. We all have to write to length, and that means pruning. Prune ruthlessly, because no one wants to spend time on words that are a waste.

The best way to prevent misunderstanding is to write in conversational language. Abandon jargon, because it limits your audience. We all use jargon. Mostly we don't know we're using it, because it is the language of our group. You only realize you're using insider expressions when you see the puzzled looks on peoples' faces.

When I left the *Wall Street Journal* for *The New York Times* to become a food writer, I was mystified by some of the words I heard—kind of surprising given that both places were in the same business. The first day I walked into the headquarters on West 43rd Street, I was shown to my desk on the fourth floor in the Style department, told to come up with a story for that week's cover of what was then called the Living section, and informed that a backfielder would handle my piece.

What was a backfielder?

I was afraid to ask. I didn't want to sound stupid. (The fear of sounding stupid keeps a lot of us from learning things we need to know.)

These days, new reporters at the *Times* will not hear the word *backfielder*, but instead will be greeted with the phrase *strong editor*. Which is weird, because it makes you immediately wonder, what do they do with the weak editors?

Every industry, every company, every town, even families have their own ways of talking, their own shorthand for communicating. When my husband answers the phone by saying, "Heddo," I know it's either his brother or sister. He is using a word that goes back to a subtle mockery of a cousin whose version of "Hello" became part of the siblings' private language. Jargon and shorthand can be fun in conversation, and a way to define group identity. It's fair to use it in talking with people who presumably know that same language.

A friend who reported for the *Journal* sometimes recounts her rocky history of writing about commodities. She remembers being brand new to the beat, put in with no time to prepare, and having to call analysts for their take on the day's events. When she asked why the cocoa market was "limit up," the analyst said, "Everyone was out there covering their shorts!" She immediately imagined a bunch of guys in white boxers racing around trying to conceal their underwear. She had no idea what the guy was talking about. It took many questions for a novice to understand the phrase "covering your shorts."

The world of business is drowning in jargon that's used so often it becomes a cliché. I was in a meeting where a smart man actually said this:

We want to take a view and put a stake in the ground because we have some skin in the game.

Wow.

Jargon is efficient in its own context, but it's mystifying when presented to the wider world. Nothing gets in the way of speaking like a human more than jargon does. To the person using it, it seems the natural way to talk. But it isn't. It's the language of science, or finance, or marketing; it is not conversational.

If words are so difficult to decode, there is no reason to wade through. The language of the financial, medical, and government worlds seems deliberately confusing. Bank accounts, mortgage statements, closing documents for house sales, insurance policies, health insurance rules—rarely are they in plain English. Paperwork is endless and confusing not because it has to be, but because it is usually written to satisfy lawyers or, more nefariously, to keep people from easily understanding their rights and responsibilities.

Legal jargon leaves people needing a lawyer to explain what should be a simple contract to buy a house or make a will. The tech industry has followed suit with agreements about the use of your

Academic writing often suffers from jargon. This example was created by Andrew Kuhn, a psychotherapist, poet, and master mimic.

> With respect to unpacking the cultural impacts of inequities, it is patent that everything from historical prevalences to metrics to semiotic valences of specific images and memes provide fodder for controversy. To take just one single instance, collective sensitivities to what the French would call a decalage between status and financial well-being do not necessarily correspond to available information about statistical disparities, let alone the "meanings" made of these. The very facticity of "facts" is at play here. While by the same token, disciplines may consider different realms of evidence under different lenses, or optics, making for a Tower of Babel of specialists speaking past each other, or out of one another's earshot altogether, as they tend to attend different conferences, read different journals, attend different parties, etcetera—even at the same institution of so-called higher learning! And who should be allowed to speak, and to or for whom? Cultural appropriation, mansplaining, and the constant threat of real or perceived micro-aggressions can offer further impedances to a fruitful exchange of views. So how to even begin a conversation about this very important topic, or topics, is problematic.

I think that in translation, that says: Academics from different disciplines have trouble talking to one another.

The federal government has a smart and useful site on plain language. Here is a "before" of government wordiness:

> If the State Secretary finds that an individual has received a payment to which the individual was not entitled, whether or not the payment was due to the individual's fault or misrepresentation, the individual shall be liable to repay to State the total sum of the payment to which the individual was not entitled.

And here is the "after," in plain language:

> If the State agency finds that you received a payment that you weren't entitled to, you must pay the entire sum back.

information that no one can follow. When it turns out that your information is being used in ways you didn't anticipate, it's because those agreements are too daunting to approach.

When I was editing opinion submissions, I saw pieces so loaded with jargon that they made sense only to people in that field. As Op-Ed editors, we shared our knowledge to translate jargon and figure out if a piece was worth saving. As one editor wrote about a submission,

> *I'd have to see it in plain English first. I mean, they had me at "The tax code's prohibition of trading in tax attributes, meanwhile, precludes developers from simply selling off their tax credits."*

This is a made-up paragraph, but it's similar to what you might find in a press release:

> Companies are increasingly leveraging technology to engage with their stakeholders. They are innovating through data-driven insights, multimedia tactics and in so doing, leveraging print, electronic, and social media as critical components of their toolkit.

This is how a business editor might translate that paragraph:

> The boring old annual report is dead. Now, companies are using social media to stay in touch with customers and shareholders.

Watch out for these overused words and phrases:

- point in time
- at the end of the day
- it's not rocket science
- impactful
- paradigm
- bandwidth
- on the same page
- under the radar
- innovate
- influence
- think outside the box
- literally

These ideas could be expressed in just one word:

- a total of
- reverts back
- free of charge
- charged in connection with
- fled the scene
- arrived at the scene
- at the end of the day
- general public

Why do people use that kind of language in the first place? It is efficient when they are talking to their peers, and they all know their verbal shorthand. The mistake is when they use that private language to talk with people outside of that circle. They will get tuned out.

We didn't end up using that particular piece, so I can't show you the translation, but it would have been a simple edit to turn that sentence into this one:

> *Developers who cannot use their tax credits get no value from them because they are not allowed to sell them.*

A small change, but it makes the idea understandable.

Financial articles were typically tough to decode and often left the editors in Op-Ed mystified. A piece sent to us by a well-known economist brought this comment from one of the editors:

> *Gurgle, gurgle. Could someone who understands this help me? Worth it, or impenetrable?*

Some articles we received relied heavily on insider language, but I wanted to save and publish them because I found the ideas worth sharing. Often the editing was easy; it just involved trimming. Maybe that's why I love both gardening and editing; I like to create a shape from something that looks blurry and a little confusing.

Theoretically, jargon should become less common as people communicate visually and through texting. Texting isn't writing; it's talking. And over time it will probably replace some of the old conventions of writing, because conversation is the more natural way to communicate and it predates writing.

In any attempt to persuade, be sure the flow of words is logical and that A definitely leads to B which leads to C. I remember a piece I was tempted to publish because it was emotional and about a subject that moved me. In the wake of her baby's death at day-care, a woman was arguing for more family leave. She believed that if her time off work had been longer, her baby would have been spared. But the logical flaw in that claim was pointed out by one of the editors, who said the baby could have died even if the mother had been at home. Her desire for more maternity leave was a goal that made sense, but the two parts of her article weren't really connected—"the baby died when she went to work, but not necessarily because she had to go to work." I hated to reject it, but the logic didn't hold.

To be sure that you have made your words simple, easy to follow, specific, and jargon free, you have to get some distance on your own writing. The best advice I can give you with that problem? Write something and go back to it the next day, first thing in the morning, before you have any other words or ideas in your head, and you will see it anew. When my own writing stumps me, when I know it's out of order or otherwise not quite right, I'm able to figure out the next day how to fix it. It always shocks me that I couldn't see it earlier.

Give your brain time to rest, and you can be your own editor.

15

Coming Up with Ideas

Finding a novel idea is the hardest part of writing. But originality is critical because people will ignore ideas and stories they have heard before.

Creative and imaginative thinking is actually quite rare. Most people, if encouraged, can find a new way to do something, but either they don't see themselves as creative or they don't get that opportunity. Research by Kyung Hee Kim suggests that the American focus on testing and controlling children, as well as frequent group activities, has brought about a steady decline in creativity over the last twenty-five years.

Editors or professors or writing coaches can work with you on executing an idea, but the creativity depends on you. You can be bright and educated and still not manage to come up with an idea that is a new twist on the prevailing conversation. Or, you can have tons of creative ideas and be unable to craft them, intelligently, into a workable piece.

At the *Times*, we knew that the success of our work rose and fell on the quality of ideas. We had regular daily meetings about the news and how we might respond. Those were quick meetings—so quick we didn't even sit down. Once a week, though, we would meet for an hour in a conference room. I asked the editors to arrive with ideas to share.

Some editors methodically looked for ideas, often by going through publishers' catalogs. I tried to read websites and publications that were directed to the specialists in the fields I followed closely, like health and business.

I don't think most people are creative in groups. But sometimes having a deadline to come up with ideas will force you to do the work that leads to creativity. It puts a structure and a practice into the process of having to think. Some of your best ideas might arrive in the shower or during a walk, but it's also possible to intentionally capture them.

At those weekly meetings, to minimize distractions, I asked people to turn off their phones and close their laptops. I knew they thought I was being ridiculous, but I wanted them to be fully present. (I've never read an article or book on productivity—and I consume a lot of them, trying to tame my procrastinating nature—that doesn't recommend leaving the phone far away so you won't be tempted to pick it up and scroll through emails or social feeds. I know that's good advice. If I leave it right next to me, it's shocking how often I look at it.)

I opened the meetings by going around the room, asking people what they were thinking about. When one editor shared an idea, the others jumped in with various ways to look at it and offered suggestions for writers. It's stressful to know that your livelihood depends on being continually original and creative. It's not as if those ideas just stream out like water from a hose. Sometimes in those meetings,

I would look around that long table and see people studying pieces of paper or trying not to make eye contact because they didn't have anything they thought was exciting. To pretend that they did, sometimes they would mention suggestions that had been sent to them for writers. They didn't need to use the meeting for that. They were just filling air. I remember one meeting where there was just silence.

Finally one of the editors, Peter Catapano, said, "I was thinking about my recycling this morning."

When I first met Peter, I thought we might have trouble working together because he so clearly didn't want to be micromanaged or told what to do, and I was the new boss. Over time I realized that he had an original mind: he came up with unusual ideas, and writers liked working with him. And when he saw that as long as he was productive, I had no interest in controlling him or regulating his days, he accepted me as the boss. If editors came up with ideas that I had never heard before, I didn't care whether they spent their time in coffee shops or in the office. I asked Peter to elaborate.

"I was trying to wash peanut butter out of a plastic container to recycle it and I was using all of this hot water, and it took like five minutes," he said. "And so I just wondered, am I doing more harm than good?"

Now, that was interesting. It's a liberal shibboleth that recycling is good, even when research sometimes shows that the benefits are mixed. It's always worth looking for an article that will question the readers' orthodoxy. We talked about the idea as a group, and Peter said he would get in touch with John Tierney, who had written about recycling when he was on staff at the *Times* before leaving to freelance and write books. I loved that idea because I had long admired Tierney's work. He was always surprising.

So, that was done.

Anything else?

A few desultory comments. Nothing else of note. But that was fine.

A meeting that produced a Sunday cover story was well worth the time. Those fifty-two articles were among the most important stories we did.

Ideas can come from multiple places. When Google, pressed to be more transparent about political advertising, released some information on who was buying what, Kendall Collins wrote an op-ed that appeared in the *Times* about the failure of Democrats to use digital ads. The Republicans were way ahead of them in understanding how to use that tool, Collins said. As a former marketing executive at Salesforce, he knew how effective digital ads could be. He was shocked to find that the average nonpresidential Democratic campaign was spending only 10 percent to 15 percent of its budget on digital channels while most of the remaining funds went to TV and mail—even though people average 5.9 hours online every day. He took a kernel of something and developed it into a surprising story.

Ideas can come to you through comments made in passing. Recently, I was at a book party when someone said that half of the world's population growth in the next few decades will occur in Africa. Really? After all those years of people worrying about population in China? That was intriguing to me. I thought someone could write a good piece based on that factoid.

As you go about your life, you'll find that someone—your doctor, the groomer for your dog, the guy at the car rental agency—says something that seems worth writing about. I can't overstate the value of putting down your phone and having conversations with people. People use screens as crutches when they are too shy to talk to people, or when they're bored. Whether you're doing a job that has nothing to do with writing or you're hoping to make writing your career, lift up your head from the screen.

Kate Murphy, who writes frequently for the *Times*, avoids social media because she doesn't want to do stories that just chew on what everyone else is talking about. Instead, she starts up conversations wherever she goes. When I told her that I wanted to discuss her idea-generating process, she told me to just look in my email for her original story pitches. I told her that when I left the *Times*, I lost access to those emails. She jumped on it. She wondered where they went, whether anyone looked at them, what happened—making it clear to me that one of these days, I'll see an article about how companies deal with the email of former employees. Her stories are often on the paper's most emailed or most viewed lists, and I think it's because she is telling people something that they haven't thought about before. She doesn't write from news conferences or pitches from public relations people. Regular people she encounters in her day-to-day life, not government officials and other journalists, are her inspiration. And they can be your sources as well, when followed up with research and study.

Once you have a wisp of an idea, do some digging to be sure your take is original. Before you can write an original take on an issue, you have to know what is known; you have to know the territory. Don't write that it's time to regulate the tech giants, when others have already been writing about that. You have to think of something that's not in the conversation, some wrinkle, some aspect. You have to know what is known and then present your own twist.

Kate Murphy explains how she found the idea for a *Times* article on the question of whether your friends really like you:

> This one had a lot of threads leading to it. And most of the threads came from just listening to people. I recall more than once hearing people complain that friends didn't reciprocate invitations to go to lunch, dinner, or the movies. The relationships felt one-sided. If they stopped calling, the "friendship" would effectively be over because the other person wouldn't make the effort to keep it going.
>
> And, of course, there's Facebook where people say they have thousands of friends and then can't get anyone to bother to show up for their birthday party. That happened to someone I know. We showed up and we were the only other couple there besides the birthday boy and his girlfriend. And then I know this other guy who has a lot of "friends" because he's always buying

You will not draw attention to your ideas if you simply repeat the accepted wisdom of one side or the other. If you do not know what the most commonly accepted version of reality is, you can't dispute it. If you don't take into account the other side, and what is known, your ideas will be dismissed much more easily. Leaving out evidence central to the opposing argument will just make it easy for people to brush you off.

Can't find something new? Then maybe don't bother, unless you are a writer of such talent that you can take a perennial—an evergreen, as they're called in the media business—and make it new and fresh.

them dinner and drinks and inviting them to his vacation homes. Finally, I often hear that someone said, "Oh Kate Murphy, yes, we're good friends." Um . . . no, we aren't. I met them like, once or twice, and didn't like them at all. I have a lot of acquaintances but there are very few people I'd call friends.

It just got me thinking what we mean when we say "friend." Who are your friends, really and truly? And then while all this was brewing in my mind, this study in *PLoS One* was published that showed rather convincingly most people don't know who their friends are. People who they thought were their friends didn't feel the same way. And what really got to me about the study was the researchers said this was useful information for managers because it suggested ways they could manipulate their employees and customers. Killed me. Hands up for who wants to be friends with the researchers. Anyone?

The essayist Tim Kreider—the one who wrote about the love of his cat—excels at this. One of the most popular stories during my time in Op-Ed was "The Busy Trap." Most of our readers probably already knew that people were complaining of being inundated and "busy," in some large part due to digital media. Tim made the story feel new by challenging the notion that everyone suddenly had a lot more to do. He gently made fun of those who were constantly saying how busy they were. He argued that they were just boasting of their importance in the world. He made the reader look at a common subject in a different way, showing them that people were choosing this state of constant busyness, a condition that he called "a hedge against emptiness."

If you can't persuade me through lyrical language or philosophical insights—and only a few can—try looking for something that will surprise your readers. Take, for instance, the minimum wage. You happen to think that having the federal government increase the minimum is a bad idea, and that states taking that route will end up hurting their economies. You think these higher wages will produce fewer jobs, and when there are fewer jobs, more people will need government help. Your readers might support the idea of a higher minimum wage, but your points might make them wonder, "Could I be wrong? Could costs go up?" You've made them think.

A recent op-ed in the *Times* grabbed me because it came with this headline: "Do Taxpayers Know They Are Handing Out Billions to Corporations?" I read it because although I knew that cities and states have long given incentives to companies to get them to locate there and not elsewhere, I had no idea that the number was as high as $80 billion or that the existence of those subsidies was hidden from taxpayers. It was information I'd never heard, and so I read to the end.

Looking at your life and thinking about how your experiences might relate to the news is another route to publishable ideas. One day I got an email from a reporter whose friend's father was a Catholic priest. She thought that perspective would help her write something useful around the news that the Pope was considering revisiting the issue of celibacy for priests. People with a connection to an editor will often offer to send something on behalf of a friend, and of course, public relations people will do it on behalf of a client. Sometimes it helps a submission stand out. But most of the time, a sharp, brief explanation of the idea will get your article the attention it wants. The reporter's friend, Benedicta Cipolla, sent me her piece. Her father had been married to her mother for forty-five years, but he was also a priest in good standing because he entered the priesthood after being married. She argued that making celibacy optional would help solve the shortage of priests by encouraging young people to become priests, knowing that they could choose later to marry.

I sent it around to my editors with this note, "Small slice of the Pope story, but I think it has potential." One editor said he thought it needed a little trimming in the middle, and he wondered if we could hear anything from a parishioner, dryly noting that in all those years, "somebody must have said something memorable about having a married priest."

Once you have your idea, go deep. I had a vivid personal experience of what happens when you don't dig beneath the surface and come up with thoughts that are not obvious. It was a cold winter weekend, and my friend Rachel was visiting. We started obsessing about how crazy it was for Aziz Ansari to be taken down in the media for sexual misconduct by a woman who obviously pursued him, agreed to sex, and then later had second thoughts about the whole episode and anonymously but publicly accused him of bad behavior. We both found it aggravating and unfair, a violation of due process and the idea that people are innocent until proven guilty. While Rachel and I cooked a big pot of curry, we ranted and she convinced me to write about it. After she left, I quickly wrote down about five hundred words on the subject. I was going to try to improve my piece the next day, but didn't bother after I read an excellent piece on the subject by Caitlin Flanagan in the *Atlantic*.

Her writing offered what mine did not: she went deep. She thought of things that I hadn't. She didn't just share some off-the-cuff thoughts. If you do that, your writing probably won't be surprising enough to be truly persuasive. Not because it breaks any of the rules I have discussed, but because it's not smart enough to make a reader think in a new way.

Unlike me, Flanagan tried to understand why the young woman hadn't just walked out of Ansari's apartment. She said the unwillingness of younger women to confront men on the spot can be ascribed to the way these women were raised. She argued that their generation had been conditioned to expect the best of men, and hers, the worst.

We made many of the same points, but Flanagan brought two important things to the idea that I did not: humor and empathy.

So, while I found the Ansari incident a scary example of overreach on a matter that was profoundly important, she pulled the reader in softly with the notion that the article was "a contribution" to a conversation.

Don't assume that all ideas have been done. You can take something classic and find a new approach, sometimes playing off of the news. One time, the essayist Sloane Crosley sent in a piece on how and why women are always apologizing. She made it fresh by tying it to a new ad campaign in the subway discouraging travelers from inconsiderate behavior.

The next time you are in a coffee shop, or the library, or watching a soccer game, look at the people. Listen to their conversations. Think about whether you're seeing something you haven't seen before. Watch a mother interact with a baby. Is she holding her phone at the same time? Would a mother twenty years ago have been talking and cooing to the baby? There's probably a story there. Ideas are all around us. You just have to look at what your fellow humans are doing, and something will occur to you.

Or, just listen. I came upon one of my best stories in the mid-eighties, when I was sitting through a tedious session at a conference for securities analysts at the Don Cesar Hotel in St. Petersburg, Florida. I listened as companies in the food business made their presentations to the financial types who studied their businesses. I was probably slumping and fidgeting from boredom. It was the time before cell phones; if it hadn't been, would I have been reading the phone and missed this moment? Because suddenly I heard one of the executives mention that the company had noticed that its customers were "grazing," and it hoped to provide food to meet that market. Grazing! I loved it. The idea that people were eating the way animals did, like cows did—I hadn't heard that before. And I figured if I hadn't, given my total immersion in food publications, few of the *Journal* readers had either. As soon as I got back to New York, I started interviewing people and produced one of my favorite stories. It was fun to introduce *Journal* readers to the notion of grazing, which soon became common slang.

So listen, and watch; and if you're ready for that moment, you can tease out something novel that will show you how satisfying writing can be.

16

How to Please Editors

I have been an editor for much of my life, so I think I know what editors want. If you're trying to get something published, in all likelihood the editor wants one of three things: to be surprised by something; to be given a new perspective on an old problem; or to be delighted and impressed by the writing.

Beyond that, editors like people who are easy to work with. People who answer their email immediately, drop whatever they are doing to answer questions, and don't complain unduly about edits. Most editors are just too busy, so the more you can do for them, the better. The editor neglected to keep a list of what was coming up? You remind her. The editor, in a revise, put in an error? You fix it, without recriminations. The easier you make her job, the more success you'll have. I'm not saying that annoying, difficult, demanding, egotistical writers don't succeed. They do, if their work is too amazing to pass up. But if you're contributing pieces occasionally and want to be asked back, be a paragon of cooperation, because plenty of other people are happy to write.

Writers find themselves rejected because their articles are too long, need too much work, or just aren't surprising enough to find an editor who will spend the time required to make something succeed. Don't make your style so dazzling that it drowns out what you are saying; one of my favorite responses to a piece from a well-known writer was, "Wow, yikes, the only word of this I really understood was *bumfuzzling*."

In any kind of opinion writing, have a clear logical argument and conclusion. If you fail to do that, editors will take the easy way out and move on to something else, because there are always other possibilities and other choices. A quiet but damning comment from an editor on a piece about to be rejected has stuck with me: "Nah. Nice piece, but inessential."

You want to be essential. Make your piece the one that doesn't need a lot of work. Whether it's a professor reading it late at night for a course or an editor at a website, you don't want to cause them work, just as you don't want to strain the readers by requiring too much effort.

Before you get discouraged by an editor who rejects your writing, remember that evaluating words is subjective. No two editors are alike. Yes, there is writing so bad that almost everyone will conclude that it doesn't succeed. But from there, it's all a matter of taste and preference. I saw that vividly one day when emailing with a *Times* friend who had edited a story with a fascinating tidbit from Bill Gates, who revealed that his favorite comic was transgender and British. I never expected to be introduced to someone like that by Gates. My friend told me that the final editor on the piece, faced with a too-long story, had wanted to cut out exactly that line.

It can be frustrating for writers to know that getting published might depend on who happens to read their piece. If you have a piece rejected, it is painful to know that the particular editor who would have loved it and fought for it was out sick that day.

Editors can sound cruel when you hear them discussing articles far from the writer's hearing. Through our shared email, the *Times* Op-Ed staff would react to what was arriving in our email inboxes. We would lump writers into categories, for ease of communication. One piece, an editor said, was "basically a mom story," while another was basically a "depressed man story." A writer who had endured a harrowing life in North Korea produced something that didn't quite speak to people. Editors felt guilty about that, but reality is reality. "Some of the details are telling," one editor wrote, "but it ends up feeling very shallow to me, which is a mean thing to say about someone who's had such a tough life. Is it better than I think?"

Editors aren't heartless, but they often have to reject people. It is better to do so quickly without getting attached. It's also best to avoid explanation. If someone asked me why a piece was rejected, I never answered. It was a matter of sanity and triage. If I answered every writer, I'd never get the Op-Ed pages out. So if you are sending out your work and not getting responses, don't assume the work is hopeless and should be trashed. It just means that editor is too busy to explain why it doesn't suit his or her particular needs on that particular day.

Although some editors had memories so strong they didn't have to Google, most of us used the skills of basic reporting to find people who might write interesting pieces for us. When Japan was hit with an earthquake and tsunami on March 11, 2011, my deputy, Sewell Chan, spent much of the night at the office trying to reach writers and novelists in Japan who might be willing to write. Within days, he had a vivid piece from the novelist Kazumi Saeki about what it was like to experience the disaster. Sewell, a relentless reporter, is the intense son of Chinese immigrants, and he has degrees from both Harvard and Oxford. While I had most of my communications by email, Sewell would have long phone conversations with writers, becoming excited by their ideas, pushing them to do more. He always felt the pain of his writers and their stories. I never cried and rarely showed emotion about personal issues, whereas Sewell, on a tough day, would come to my office to talk; and if he was feeling upset for one of our staffers or for some tragedy somewhere in the world, his eyes would well up. Much more similar to me in style was Honor Jones, a gifted editor who taught me a lot about how to assess opinion pieces. Although decades apart, we had nearly identical backgrounds, editing styles, taste in fiction, and reactions to proposed articles. Maybe it was all those years on horseback.

I liked the varied personalities among my editors and thought that was one reason Op-Ed was fun. The noun *op-ed*, meaning "opposite editorial," originated in 1970 when the *Times* introduced the Op-Ed page. But today, *op-ed* is widely used to describe a particular type of short-form persuasive writing. And it's a form that many people want to master, from college students to chief executives to Nobel Prize winners. When I was in Op-Ed, we had eight Nobel Prize winners write for us, including Joseph Stiglitz, Desmond Tutu, and Amartya Sen.

Most days in Op-Ed began with a 10:30 a.m. meeting to talk about ideas and the news. In theory, the editors had to arrive at 10 a.m. and start reading the news, looking for stories that merited an opinionated reaction. But that was the old, pre-web reality. Few of us waited until 10 in the morning to start thinking about the news. Most of the editors had read the news sites the night before when fresh stories were posted online. Some of us had been emailing one another since 7 a.m. or even earlier, talking about ideas. I had no right to ask anyone who wasn't in management to start that early; but if they offered, I didn't try to stop them. If that meant they disappeared to take a son or daughter to the dentist in the middle of the day, I didn't mind. We weren't staffed to be a twenty-four-hour opinion operation—yet in reality, we had to be one.

I often started that morning meeting by mentioning something I had noticed, and then others would jump in. We tried to think of perspectives that hadn't been published and come up with names of likely writers. Our published work was a mix of articles we sought and articles that arrived unsolicited. Thinking of ideas and then suggesting names of possible writers was a big part of that meeting. We had to find angles that the newsroom wouldn't pursue, and think far enough ahead that anything we found from an academic or expert wouldn't seem old by the time it was written and edited. I would turn to one of my regular contributors like Pamela Druckerman, Jennifer Weiner, or Steven Rattner if they seemed like the best person to react to the news. After twenty or thirty minutes of debating ideas, we would return to our desks to get in touch with writers.

Throughout the day, we would read submissions both solicited and unsolicited. When there was finally a consensus about a piece we were batting around in Op Discuss, our internal email group, we used shorthand to signal where things stood: NMR meant "no more readers," as in "This piece won't work, and no more readers are needed." If my staff liked it and I did too, I'd say, "Let's schedule it."

You learn so much from the process of analyzing the work of others. If you want to improve your own writing, find examples of the form that interests you and immerse yourself in it until something about its structure winds its way into your unconscious. Read writing that is popular, and try to figure out why it works. If you want to write a speech, look up great speeches.

How to Write and Pitch an Op-Ed

Know what has run and find a different angle. Often the secret to getting an editor's attention is to approach something in a different way. If you want to write about why asthma medicine costs so much—well, that's been done. But if you refashion the piece as one about a doctor who is at odds with his own medical society over this issue so central to care, that angle might be different enough to break through.

Make an argument and offer a solution. Let's say you are writing that football players shouldn't kneel during the national anthem. Tell me why stopping them is not a violation of their free speech, and tell me what course of action their bosses should pursue. You need to offer an opinion, not just an analysis of the problem or applause for someone else's solution. Your opinion must be clear, and more than an affirmation of something that the audience already agrees with.

I remember getting an op-ed from a group of chief executives who bemoaned the lack of tech talent available and praised a city effort to provide more computer science education. That doesn't make a persuasive piece; it's not surprising, and it doesn't go beyond the news. It was thick with words that put people to sleep, like *diversity, initiative*, and *collaboration*. And it was devoid of stories about real people.

Focus. Make sure that your story has a central point, sharply rendered. The editor will want to write the headline, but if you're trying to be sure you have kept the piece tight and to the point, try writing a headline for it. If you have trouble doing that, it is not yet focused enough on a central point that is easy to explain. So keep editing yourself until you can compose a headline that pleases you.

Get to your main idea quickly. Many years ago, I got the best advice on how to write a story for the *Wall Street Journal* from my friend John Emshwiller, whom I had known from the *Daily Californian* at Berkeley. He began working at the *Journal* after college and helped me get hired. I was trying to write a page one story after spending weeks reporting it. The mass of stuff that I had to make simple, seamless, and interesting was overwhelming. I stayed up late, night after night, struggling. Finally, I asked John what I should do. He said this: Start out with what you would tell someone at a party. What is the most interesting thing? That advice was a revelation, and it changed the way I looked at the structure of that article and many of those that followed. I especially thought of John and his advice when I was in Op-Ed, where I saw too many smart people trying to bury their most interesting thought because they didn't think it seemed right to start with it.

If it's timely, you've got to be fast. The moment passes quickly. If you are trying to persuade an editor to run something you have just written, don't delay. Don't fiddle in pursuit of perfection. Do it fast, and send it. You don't want to have written the third piece that comes in that day on some development in cybertechnology, because the editors might already have decided to take the first one. If it is an anniversary or an event, submit your piece at least two weeks early. By doing that, you will make things easier for the editor and preempt those who wait until four days before the anniversary to file.

Think about order. Editors spend a lot of time rethinking and reorganizing articles. Writers often don't have the best perspective on what they know and may not understand what would be most appealing to the general reader. Our virtual conversations in Op-Ed were frequently about the order of things: How fast or how slowly did the writer get to something we considered crucial? Often when looking at a draft of an op-ed for a client or a friend, I like the idea and the writing, but the order doesn't seem right, and I just move the paragraphs around until they flow easily into one another. Because I have distance on the piece, it is easy to fix. The best order is usually the one that you would use if you were telling the story to someone in person.

Clichés and jargon will doom you. As in all persuasive writing, as I have said, you must avoid clichés and jargon. But that's even more important when you're submitting to Op-Ed editors. Editors are probably more sensitive to clichés than readers are, because they are reading all day long. I remember a submission from an impressive, accomplished athlete who relied on tired words. By the end, one editor said, "I felt like I'd swum through a 110-mile anthology of clichés."

Avoid the obvious. A piece by a famous novelist was rejected because he was writing in defense of banned books. For a liberal audience that doesn't believe in banning books, there is nothing to make you click on that idea. As one editor said, "'In defense of banned books' is the easiest, limpest op-ed topic I can think of, particularly during Banned Book Week, which is a thing?" That piece got the dreaded NMR. I always felt sorry for writers when I saw that.

Don't be blatantly self-promotional. You can write something that indirectly benefits your business or grows out of your professional knowledge, but you have to make your connection clear. For instance, Ezekiel J. Emanuel often writes about health care for the *Times*, and whenever he touches on any aspect of the Affordable Care Act—commonly known as Obamacare—he discloses that he worked on that bill for the president. That's allowed. But you can't sell an op-ed on, say, the amazing benefits of your new online clothing business. Because even if there are social benefits—maybe your clothes are for overweight women, who have few choices in stores—it will read like advertising for your brand.

How do you know whether something is ready to send to an editor or to your teacher? If it's a short piece, look at the basics. Is it focused clearly on one or two points? Is it logically told, so that a reader doesn't stop short and say, "I already read about that two paragraphs ago"? Is it original, and based on something you know or are expert in? And does it track? You never want your reader to think, "I have to reread that; I don't quite get it," because that reader will then be tempted to wander off and do something more rewarding.

If you make every effort to please the reader, you will inevitably find an editor who wants to publish your work.

PART V

The Psychology of Persuasion

17

We Believe What We Believe

We all cling to our ideas and beliefs, which makes it tough to change opinion. We all tend to think we're smart and well informed, and we're confident about our points of view. We resist other perspectives not because we are stupid and narrow-minded, but because there are fundamental psychological reasons for protecting our positions.

All of us, whether we're conservatives or liberals, dislike having our positions challenged. It makes us uncomfortable, and we perceive it as a threat. We are better at finding the holes in other people's arguments than at seeing the weaknesses in our own. Psychologists have found that we pay more attention to evidence that supports our beliefs, and we ignore evidence that goes against them—a tendency called confirmation bias. Because we seek out information that confirms what we already believe, our opinions tend to get stronger over time. We enjoy being around those who share our opinions.

We look for that community in real life and online. Paul Krugman is a wildly popular *New York Times* columnist and Nobel Prize–winning economist whose passionate readers comment frequently.

Most of those readers agree with him—and most of the time, they are commenting because they want to be part of a community that thinks the same way.

Not only do we seek out information that supports what we believe, we put much more effort than might be considered rational into trying to rebut views that emotionally disturb us. When our confidence in those beliefs is challenged, we are likely to advocate even more strongly for them.

This tribalism, this pushing away of anything that seems intellectually threatening, might seem like an irrational way to approach the world, but it is not. We are more likely to survive if we share the opinions of a group, so confirmation bias would have provided evolutionary benefits. We cling to our views because they identify us to the outside world as being part of a group. By defining who we are and keeping us safe from outsiders, our opinions end up protecting and helping us.

Many of us take on the political coloration of our families and never change. Others take on the values and ideas of our peers. We all need to be part of a tribe, and when necessary, we will mask some of our beliefs if they put us at odds with our group. If my friend who belongs to a country club in a small town dominated by Republicans is open-minded enough to read the data on climate change, he will nevertheless remain silent at the postgame drink when his friends make fun of those who rant about rising seas. His peers might not believe in the urgency of climate change. If he remains silent, he loses nothing and possibly gains. More important, he isn't doing anything to hurt efforts to deal with changing climate; if he appeared to disagree with his friends, though, he would be hurting himself.

Many have criticized how we all live in our own bubbles today, but there are unassailable reasons for people to hang around with others who feel as they do about the big issues of their day. There is safety in numbers, and it is psychological and sometimes even physical. (And if you don't feel that you fit in with the group that you find at work, or even the family you were born into, the odds are good that you will move on and find people who are more compatible.)

When you establish commonality, you end up adopting the ideas of those who make up that community. Identifying with a group and trying to make it even larger also then increases its odds of becoming the ruling group in society. When we choose our friends, we are to a degree choosing our ideas, because we become some combination of all of them. If you think your friends support a certain policy—say that cutting taxes, by helping corporations, will end up helping all workers—you're more likely to support that notion too. If there is an idea that you associate with people unlike you, then you will be more dubious of it.

Most people don't base their opinions on detailed readings of experts who have studied an issue, although they might believe that they do. Our beliefs aren't formed through a rigorous reading of information both for and against a particular issue. It's much more emotional than that. The New York University psychologist Jonathan Haidt argues that we start with feeling and then find the reasons to support what we already believe.

Haidt, author of *The Righteous Mind: Why Good People Are Divided by Politics and Religion* (2012), has shown that familiarity lessens divisions. A student is more likely to become friends with the student whose dorm room is one door away than with the student whose room is four doors away. That matters in a larger, social way, because Haidt's research also suggests that people who have at least one friend from the other political party are less likely to hate the supporters of that party. As people become more familiar to us, we tend to like them more. That even extends to furniture—you will like your new couch more the longer you have it—and to animals. The dog you at first found unappealing? Proximity leads to affection, and now you take pictures of her, admiring the odd way she crosses her back legs. We're biologically hardwired to follow others. We like to think we're individuals, but that's not how we make decisions. We like to conform to what those in our tribe are doing and thinking. To avoid standing out as freaks. We assume what other people are doing is the correct behavior in a situation. It's one of the ways we learn how to behave.

People are more likely to say yes when they see other people doing something. They might not even know them. It's why we want to eat in the restaurant with the long line, and not the one with just a few people, and why the celebrity endorsement is powerful. A study by Noah J. Goldstein, Robert Cialdini, and Vladas Griskevicius showed that people were more likely to reuse their towels in a hotel and not request that they be washed every day when they were told that most of their fellow hotel guests had done that. Group influence is powerful. Even if you don't know your fellow travelers in the hotel, just the fact that you're all staying there puts you in the same group.

Most of us dislike uncertainty, and so we come up with explanations for whatever happens, and we hold on to them no matter what. People with a high need for closure make decisions quickly and resist more information. People with a low need for closure can accept much more ambiguity—and might have trouble making decisions. But whether we need closure may depend on circumstances. The social psychologist Arie Kruglanski has found that we all need more closure in times of stress and flux. For instance, he and his researchers saw that as the terrorism threat increased after September 11, support for President George W. Bush grew. People didn't like feeling uncertain, and so they were more likely to agree with the president's decision that something had to be done, even if that something was an attack against Iraq.

Ideology, once it takes hold, is powerful. In his book *The Political Brain: The Role of Emotion in Deciding the Fate of the Nation* (2007), the psychologist Drew Westen wrote about an experiment in which researchers took pictures of peoples' brains as they watched videos of their preferred candidates in an election. In the videos, their candidate contradicted prior positions. As soon as the test participants realized the contradiction, the part of their brain that handles logic stopped working. They needed to keep out information that presented a problem. Other researchers have noticed our refusal to accept information that could be challenging. Holding fast to our positions makes people—well—a bit stupid. Dan Kahan, a professor of law and psychology at Yale, has found that both liberals and conservatives analyzed and answered problems regarding climate change in such a way that guaranteed they would get the answers that emotionally resonated with them. In effect, their greater intelligence and critical reasoning skill, rather than driving members of those groups to converge on the best scientific evidence, magnified polarization on whether human beings were contributing to global warming.

The depth of our desire to avoid other points of view was demonstrated in a series of studies led by Jeremy Frimer at the University of Winnipeg. In one study the researchers recruited 202 Americans online and divided them into two groups, those for and those against same-sex marriage. Participants were informed that if they chose to read information in support of their position and then answer questions, they would win $7.00. If they chose to read information against their position, they would win $10.00. Most people in this study were so eager to avoid the opposite point of view that they passed up the chance to win more money. Liberals and conservatives were equally strong in their desire to avoid information that might challenge their views. The scientists repeated the experiment with another 245 Americans and got similar results. And they found the same results with other issues. People just generally wanted to hear from people who agreed with them on questions ranging from important political ones to minor day-to-day decisions, like whether to have a Pepsi or a Coke.

Why do we stick so tenaciously to our views? It's partly because we don't want to try to hold two opposing beliefs in our mind. And it's partly because we just don't find it pleasant to acknowledge that we all hold such different ideas. People don't like to regret their choices. It's not in us. We don't want to see evidence that a decision we made might have been mistaken, so we just choose not to see. No one wants to put aside their own ideas. It takes effort. At the same time, we don't understand why other people don't walk away from beliefs we find so obviously wrongheaded.

It's much more psychologically comfortable to stick with our beliefs.

You don't simply believe what you believe forever. People do change. We might ignore overwhelming evidence that a certain notion is wrong for a period of time that seems incomprehensible, but eventually we will no longer be able to bear the contrast between what we want to believe and what is clearly true. So we flip.

Even if you succeed in changing someone's mind, don't expect them to admit that they changed their beliefs. They will even lie to themselves to protect the sanctity of their belief, as voters did in the 1960s. John F. Kennedy barely won the popular vote for president. And yet, after he was assassinated, millions of people decided that they had voted for him—64 percent of the people told pollsters that Kennedy got their vote. Because their sense of the correct belief had changed, they rewrote their own history.

18

The Power of Moral Values

Arthur Brooks is a passionate Christian and a passionate capitalist who believes that free markets are the best way to lift up all people, especially the poor. But he understands that in some quarters, his endorsement of capitalism makes him suspect. And, when he was a regular opinion contributor to *The New York Times*, he knew there were many liberals in that audience who probably disagreed with him on most matters.

During the time I edited his monthly column, while Arthur was president of the American Enterprise Institute, I was always impressed by his ability to find common ground. Here's a good example: When he decided to write a column about the lack of conservative faculty on American campuses, he didn't call liberals hypocrites for rejecting conservatives from jobs. He warmed up his audience.

He aligned himself with the typical liberal conviction that diversity is a good thing. Although I suspect he does this intuitively, he followed all the rules of persuasion: he empathetically established a bond with his audience, showed that he cared about the same things, and then introduced an idea that, based on that shared value system, should resonate with the audience.

He kind of tricked them, though. After establishing that they all wanted the same thing, he quoted a new study that found that for every politically conservative social psychologist in academia, there are about fourteen liberal social psychologists. He wrote that the study's researchers found evidence of discrimination and hostility within academia toward conservative researchers and their viewpoints. And in one survey, an overwhelming 79 percent of social psychologists admitted they would be less likely to support hiring a conservative colleague than a liberal scholar with equivalent qualifications.

That was a smart move by Arthur, because it played on a core moral value of liberals: fairness. So what is the liberal reader to do? Say it's okay to discriminate against conservatives? Not likely. It's impossible to know how many minds Arthur changed with that article, but I can cite at least one: my own. That clever combination of playing on a moral value and then showing how it was not being applied made me see the matter in a new way.

In that essay, Arthur used one of the most important tactics in persuasion: address your audience from the perspective of their values and morals, not yours. It's impossible to overstate the importance of moral perspectives. Some research suggests that your morals and values influence your ideas and your votes more than gender, race, wealth, education, or party affiliation.

People have strong feelings about what makes a good life and a good society, and they support viewpoints that confirm those feelings. If you don't understand the moral framework of your audience, you can't be convincing. You can't expect someone to change their basic values, so you have to make your argument in a way that fits with their values.

Liberals and conservatives are associated with different moral values. In general, liberals endorse equality and fairness while conservatives support loyalty, patriotism, respect for authority, and moral purity. Republicans are associated with the sacred and Democrats with the secular, with material interests. Some psychologists trace the value differences to parenting, arguing that strict parenting and personal insecurity turn people against liberality and diversity. For conservatives, equality and personal autonomy are less important than the values of the families and family roles.

Sociologists have found that arguments are more likely to be accepted when they are framed in a way that comports with the moral values of the audience. But doing that is challenging. People typically present their arguments from their own moral perspectives because they don't know any other way to persuade. It takes a real leap to put yourself inside the head of your audience and thoroughly take on its perspective.

Robb Willer, a professor at Stanford, and Matthew Feinberg, an assistant professor at the University of Toronto, did numerous studies showing that people are more likely to accept arguments framed to acknowledge their values. Their studies showed how tough it is for people to make an argument from their audience's point of view.

When Willer and Feinberg asked liberals to write a persuasive argument for same-sex marriage that would convince a conservative, and offered a cash prize, only 9 percent of them made their case by appealing to conservative values. They wrote from their own values of fairness. If they had wanted to persuade conservatives, they should have emphasized values like patriotism and group loyalty, saying for instance that "same-sex couples are proud and patriotic Americans." Conservatives had the same blind spot. When asked to write an argument to a liberal audience in favor of making English the official U.S. language, only 8 percent of them could do it using the moral framework of liberals; 59 percent based their argument on conservative values.

In a similar experiment, Willer and Feinberg wanted to see what it would take to persuade liberals to support greater military spending. One message argued that we should "take pride in our military." The other argued that military spending is necessary because through the military, poor and disadvantaged people can "achieve equal standing" and escape poverty. Liberals were much more likely to support more spending if they read the message about fairness than the one appealing to patriotism.

Values like these have major consequences in politics and public life. George Lakoff, for many years a professor of linguistics at the University of California at Berkeley and the author of *Don't Think of an Elephant! Know Your Values and Frame the Debate* (2004), argues that Republicans have been much smarter than Democrats about marketing and reaching people through their moral values. Lakoff believes Democrats have suffered for their conviction that facts are the route to persuasion, a point of view embodied in the eighteenth-century Enlightenment. Progressives, he says, need to make their messages positive, reinforce what they are saying, and avoid helping those with whom they disagree. Lakoff describes that process as changing the frame through which people view an issue or an argument.

Here's how George Lakoff would change the framing of a message:

> *When anti-immigrant politicians say:* "Immigrants are [negative label]."
>
> *Respond by saying:* "Immigrants are [positive label]."
>
> *Examples:* "Immigrants are our neighbors." "Immigrants are our families." "Immigrants are our heroes."
>
> *Never say:* "Immigrants are not [negative label]."

The same goes for environmental issues.

> *When fossil fuel companies say:* "Coal is [positive label]."
>
> *Respond by saying:* "Coal is [negative label]."
>
> *Examples:* "Coal is dirty." "Coal is dangerous." "Coal is harmful."
>
> *Never say:* "Coal is not [positive label]."

Always say what you believe, directly. Whatever the issue or argument at hand, remember that the word *not* generally ensures you will repeat your opponent's argument and make it more likely to stick in the brains of your listeners.

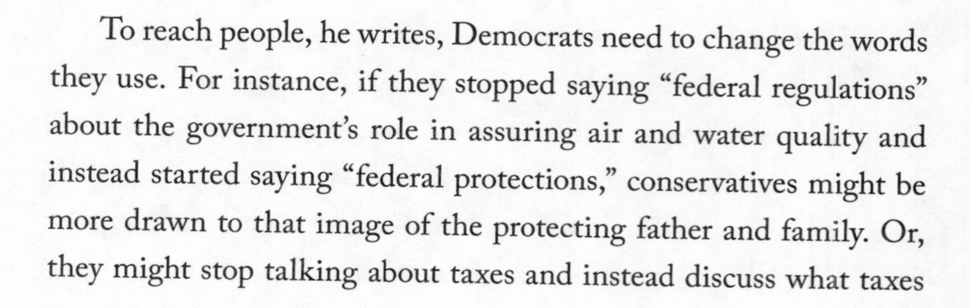

To reach people, he writes, Democrats need to change the words they use. For instance, if they stopped saying "federal regulations" about the government's role in assuring air and water quality and instead started saying "federal protections," conservatives might be more drawn to that image of the protecting father and family. Or, they might stop talking about taxes and instead discuss what taxes are for—say, "investments in public resources," so that people would understand that the government pays for what we all use—schools, roads, bridges, courts, and the like.

Is it shocking that liberals and conservatives approach the world with different values? It shouldn't be. Look at the people you're trying to reach, and put yourself where they are. Thinking about what they care about, as Arthur did with his article on discrimination against conservatives in faculty appointments, will help you have a better chance of changing a mind or two.

19

What Really Changes People

It's tough to define exactly what transforms the way someone sees the world.

I can only look at my own life and guess at what made me shift away from my Republican family and adopt viewpoints that were different from theirs.

I had grown up feeling perpetually guilty about the inequality that confronted me. My mother had always had a housekeeper. Until she married my stepfather when I was fourteen, I never saw her do any domestic work, and yet I grew up in a house where the beds were made with crisp corners, light summer blankets were topped with perfectly ironed monogrammed covers, and silver was always polished. My mother worked in her family's business, but I didn't know what she did there, and she rarely talked about it.

Who was doing all that housework? It was Margaret Weiss, who we called Margie. She had started college but had to drop out when her family lost its money during the Depression. She had wanted to be a home economics teacher. Instead she became a housekeeper, first for my mother's parents and then for my mother.

Watching my mother and Margie taught me lessons that have stayed with me. One, hard work doesn't always pay. Margie had free room and board and earned a pittance. My mother also had free room and board, just by being born into a certain family. Two, money doesn't guarantee happiness. Margie was happy. I knew her throughout her life, long after she stopped working for my mother. Thanks to her three successful children, she had a nice retirement. My mother, until she married a second time, always seemed discontented.

I was emotionally primed to become someone who did not believe that we all make our own lives through our own skill and hard work. To be a liberal.

How does change happen for others? My friend Arthur Brooks was born into a liberal family in Seattle and evolved into a conservative Catholic. It's as if he and I switched places politically, and yet we have similar values and I admire him unreservedly.

Arthur's conversion to Catholicism began when he was fifteen and visited the shrine to Our Lady of Guadalupe during a school trip to Mexico. He looked up at the image of the Blessed Virgin and felt like Mary was appearing to him. A few months later, he started the conversion process in Seattle.

His Protestant parents weren't thrilled; but they figured Catholicism was probably better than drugs, which he had started using in eighth grade. His next conversion was professional. In his mid-twenties, Arthur was a bohemian and a musician living in Barcelona, holding progressive political views: "I fancied myself a social justice warrior and regarded capitalism with a moderately hostile predisposition. I 'knew' what everyone knows: Capitalism is great for the rich but terrible for the poor," he wrote in an article for *America* magazine when describing his two conversions.

But when Arthur resumed his college education by taking correspondence courses, he learned while studying economics that 2 billion people had escaped poverty in his lifetime. What's more, virtually all development economists agreed, that feat had been accomplished through globalization, free trade, property rights, the rule of law, and the culture of entrepreneurship. He became an acolyte for the American free enterprise system. He quit music, got a PhD in policy analysis, and taught economics and social entrepreneurship before taking over at American Enterprise Institute, a Washington think tank that promotes capitalism.

We met because I was looking for conservative voices for the Op-Ed page, and he offered to have coffee with me. Instantly I was taken with his warmth, his brain, and his ability to write without jargon and obfuscation.

I'm interested in what changes people. I've asked a lot of them whether they can identify something they believe that they didn't always believe, and asked them to tell me what changed them. Many people can't think of anything. Their ideas become so much a part of them that they can't remember when or how changes happened.

I can think of cases where I was influenced by facts, but most of the changes I've experienced have been gradual. Shortly after moving to New York, I completely adopted the idea shared by my friends that rent control and rent stabilization were a good thing and the only way to keep apartments affordable in the city. But when I became friends with an economics professor at NYU, I found that he had a different perspective. He thought the regulations were unfair because they didn't help people with the least amount of money; they helped people who happened to get to the city first, and then discouraged them from moving. They were imprisoned by their good deals. I was intrigued and began to think about what he had said—that poor people weren't the intended beneficiaries of rent supports—when my other friends brought up the rent issue. I didn't change my opinion overnight, but I did start to look at it in a more nuanced way.

Social science researchers, and philosophers before them, have some idea of what changes people, but they don't expect simple steps or instant results. Sometimes change has to occur in person, person by person. Sometimes change is spread through the media, rapid and astonishing, like the "me too" moment that is putting sexual harassment and the work lives of women in front of the nation and ending the careers of many powerful men.

Here are some of the top takeaways on what works, from decades of research and studies by multiple experts in the field.

Some of the suggestions based on academic research apply only in one-on-one discussions—when you might, for instance, want to get your wife to do a better job of picking up her clothes—whereas others will work in writing or speaking. Some of these ideas have been touched on directly or indirectly in preceding chapters, but I think it's helpful to have them in one list.

What Experts Find Persuasive

Give someone something. If you can figure out what people desire and make sure they get it, they'll be much more likely to give you what you want. Even a small gift makes people more likely to do what you want them to do. People like to get presents, and they want to reciprocate. That's why we had such strict rules at the *Times* and the *Journal* forbidding us from accepting gifts. I remember receiving a gorgeous smoked duck at the *Journal*; the gift was impossible to send back, so I sent it to a charity. I made exceptions only for flowers, because I figured they would go to waste. But even then, I put them out in the middle of the room so they wouldn't be on my desk reminding me that a certain person was trying to get me to do something.

Just ask. Lots of us hate to ask for anything, so we just don't do it. That's a big mistake. Asking doesn't hurt. Studies show that people underestimate the odds that someone will say yes to a direct request.

Be humble. When you qualify what you're saying, you are admitting that you might not know all that can be known. This is like saying you are willing to listen. If you say, "That could be true," it's easier for your listeners to agree with you. Think about the words you use when you need to lessen antagonism because you're writing for an audience with viewpoints different from yours.

If you tell a colleague, "You should have finished that by now," that person will naturally become defensive. But if you say, "I am stressed because that work isn't done," you are removing the accusation.

Researchers have also found that if you say a person's name more often, you are more likely to win their affection or trust.

See the value in becoming friendly with people who have different viewpoints. It will make all of us smarter and more flexible. You might not be able to change the world, but you can change yourself, a little, by reaching out. Start a conversation by pointing out something that you or your side was wrong about. That immediately takes the discussion out of combat mode.

Make people explain their positions. Academics have shown that people push themselves to think critically only when they know they will have to explain themselves to people who are well informed.

This means that if you are in a discussion or a debate, you need to force the other people to explain what they think. Ask how they would turn their ideas into policy, or how they think some current law works. If you try to get someone to walk you through her point of view and she can't quite do it, she will see the holes in her argument and possibly be more open to what you have to say. When people can't explain why they believe what they believe, they tend to ratchet down the intensity of their opinions.

Use charts and graphs. In a 2018 study, the political scientists Brendan Nyhan and Jason Reifler wanted to understand why Americans hold so many misperceptions. They tried to find out if providing correct information would cure people of their mistaken beliefs.

In several tests, they found that graphs and charts are more effective than text in helping people absorb information. Nevertheless, even the best formatted information runs up against resistance because people reject notions that threaten their self-worth. The two found that although self-affirmation exercises occasionally made people more open, their value was not as strong as prior research in the field had indicated.

Inform people of the socially accepted consensus. People want to be like other people and conform to social standards. If you show them there is a consensus around a certain idea, and you avoid being confrontational, your audience is more likely to come around to accepting that consensus.

Understand what people fear. People's political beliefs are affected by what they fear, and how fearful they are. Political psychology research shows that conservatives react more strongly to physical threats than liberals do. Their concern with physical safety was probably determined early in their lives.

That's why liberal politicians suggest to the public that danger is manageable. Republicans, though, are more likely to emphasize the risk of immigration or terrorism because jacking up fear helps them get votes.

Similarly, researchers have shown that when people were made to feel afraid about the flu, they were more likely to be against immigration, and when they were made to feel safer about the flu, their fears about immigrants abated. Our ideas are influenced by unconscious motivations that can be accessed by people who want to influence us.

Create friction to reduce bad habits, and eliminate friction to introduce good ones. We all take the easiest path. That's not lazy, it's just human nature. Anything that makes a choice even slightly easier draws people. We eat grapes at parties because we can pop them so easily into our mouths, and cookies at buffets rather than big messy slices of pie. Frictionless.

If you want to persuade someone to stop doing something, make it hard for them to do it, not easy. Smoking rates in the United States declined when there were fewer and fewer places to smoke. Eventually, it's not worth the trouble when you have to leave your desk, take an elevator, and stand outside in 20-degree weather. Do you want people to drink more water and less soda? Make sure machines stock water. Want to stop eating so much sugar? Don't keep any at home. If you have to drive to the supermarket for a teaspoon of sugar for your tea, you probably won't do it. You want to socialize more? Have some standing dinner dates. Then you don't have to go to the trouble of organizing it each time. Want to reduce time spent on social media? Take the apps off your phone.

Be warm and friendly. Make people like you. Compliment them. We all respond to compliments. People like to say yes to people they like, and they're much more able to say no to people they don't like. People need to talk about what they have in common before they tackle points of disagreement.

Sneak past emotional barriers. You need to avoid getting people upset if you want to get them to hear your ideas. You need to sidle up to them to get past the resistance that people naturally erect.

Target your audience through its values. Do not judge. Understand who you are addressing, and tailor your work to that. Let's say you are trying to persuade the last holdout in your family to quit smoking. Research suggests that if you connect that behavior change to some crucial part of a person's identity, you might make more progress. So, if you push the idea that someone will be a good person, father, member of the community—whatever your audience holds most dear—then you are more likely to succeed in changing behavior. For some people, believing they could live longer would be influential; for others, that's too abstract, and they would be more likely to change by thinking about how their premature death would leave their family bereft. Connect the behavioral change to a central part of a person's identity. That might require a number of efforts. It's not easy to dislodge a long-held idea or habit.

Show confidence and authority. It's tough to be both humble and confident, but it can be done. You need to show calm confidence.

Never repeat a falsehood. Reframe the argument so that you are not repeating the one you disagree with or helping to spread falsehoods.

Seek small steps, minimal effort. Call for small steps. I feel gloomy about a warming climate and can't imagine what I can do about it. But if someone could convince me that I could do some little thing that would make a difference, I would definitely be persuaded. That's why I've been faithfully recycling all these years, and trying not to use paper towels, even though both of those actions at a larger scale might be meaningless. I feel they make a difference, so I do them.

These ideas are just a few that have come out of social science research. The field is constantly evolving, and it's fun to keep up with what is being discovered about our all-too-human natures.

CODA:
GO FORTH!

In writing this book, I have read lots of studies on persuasion. And interestingly, many of them presented in a structured way what I had come to see experientially and anecdotally in my work as an editor.

But sometimes, the sheer weight of so many experts talking about the challenge of persuasion left me demoralized. Were all those long days in Op-Ed worth it? Can you change people's minds?

So one day, while thinking about that question, I called Alexander Coppock, an assistant professor of political science at Yale. He had recently done a study on something near to my heart and experience: He wanted to know whether op-eds made any difference at all—were they worth all the time and, indirectly, the money that went into them? Coppock had designed an online study that surveyed thousands of people, dividing them into a control group and one "treated" with op-eds. He found that those who read the op-ed material were more likely to agree with the author's perspective than those who did not read it.

He says no one really knows what makes people change their

minds—he and his collaborators from the Cato Institute simply found that people *were* influenced, not *why*. Both Republicans and Democrats changed in equal measure, agreeing with the author by about 5 to 10 percentage points more after reading the article. The "treatment" with written ideas didn't produce radical changes, like converting a Democrat into a Republican, but the changes were measurable and sustained.

I have faith in the power of persuasion, mainly because I have seen so much positive change over my life. Engaging with the world, whether through writing or in person, is what the world *is*, what life is. I hope these chapters have given you the inspiration and the confidence to go out and write. It's satisfying to pull together your thoughts and share them. We are all in this together, and our words connect us in the most primal and profound way.

ACKNOWLEDGMENTS

I owe thanks to many people, but first and most important to my editor, Robert Weil. He was confident enough to take a chance on this book and kind enough not to give up on me when the first draft was flawed. I've never encountered such a dedicated, smart, committed editor.

Then there is Alice Martell, my agent. In all the years I have known her, this is only my second book, so she's hardly getting rich off me. She is a steadfast friend and adviser.

The idea for this book came from Arthur Brooks, one of the most enjoyable writers I have ever edited. When I was whining to Arthur that I didn't know what I wanted to do with my life, post Op-Ed, he suggested that I do this.

I am indebted to Andy Rosenthal, who gave me such an amazing opportunity. To all of my colleagues at the *Times* Op-Ed department: I will never stop being grateful for what you taught me and for how satisfying those five years were.

Finally, I want to thank my husband, Larry Wolhandler; our daughter, Hally Wolhandler; and the many great friends and relatives who made it possible for me to have a happy life.

INDEX